ARISTOTLE'S

A PRIMER ON ARISTOTLE

CU00649539

I saw the Master there of those who know,
Amid the philosophic family,
By all admired, and by all reverenced;
There Plato too I saw, and Socrates,
Who stood beside him closer than the rest.

Dante, *The Divine Comedy, Inferno IV*

ARISTOTLE'S UNIVERSE
A PRIMER ON ARISTOTLE

Neel Burton
BSc, MBBS, MRCPsych, MA (Phil), AKC

Acheron Press
Flectere si nequeo superos
Acheronta movebo

© Neel Burton 2011

Published by Acheron Press

All rights reserved. No part of this book may be reproduced or transmitted, in any form or by any means, without permission.

A CIP catalogue record for this book is available from the British Library.

ISBN 978 0 9560353 5 6

Typeset by Phoenix Photosetting, Chatham, Kent, United Kingdom
Printed and bound by SRP Limited, Exeter, Devon, United Kingdom

Cover image of the helix nebula courtesy of NASA

Preface

Following in the footsteps of *Plato's Shadow*, this book aims to provide a succinct précis of the most important or influential works in the Aristotelian corpus. This should enable the student or general reader not only to survey Aristotle's principle arguments, but also to locate and to appreciate them in the context of his broader worldview. This worldview gradually reveals itself through the Master's accumulated works, which, though well worth reading, amount to some three or four thousand pages of often dense and disjointed prose. So much so, in fact, that I must apologise if my interpretation occasionally verges on the eccentric or erroneous, or if I have left out too many minor arguments and finer distinctions. I have already spent far too much time in the preparation of this book; any more and I shall surely lose my eyesight.

Neel Burton
Oxford, July 2011

Contents

SECTION 1 – INTRODUCTION

I. Life of Aristotle

The man was born, he worked, and then died.

Martin Heidegger, *lecturing on Aristotle*

Aristotle was born in 384 BC at Stageira in Chalcidice, a Grecian colony in the Macedonian region of north-eastern Greece. In 348, Stageira was occupied and destroyed by Philip II of Macedon. Philip later rebuilt the city and freed its inhabitants from slavery in honour of Aristotle, who had been his childhood friend, and whom he had appointed as tutor to his son, the future Alexander the Great.

The Stagirite's father, Nicomachus, was the personal physician to King Amyntas of Macedon, the father of Philip, and the profession of medicine was quasi hereditary in his family. His mother, Phaestis, was a woman of aristocratic descent, and he also had one sister, Arimneste, and one brother, Arimnestus. Both 'Arimneste' and 'Arimnestus' translate as 'Greatly remembered', and the parallelism of these names suggests that Aristotle may have been the youngest of the three siblings. Arimneste married Proxenus of Atarneus and had a daughter, Hero, and a son, Nicanor. Hero in turn had a son, the historian Callisthenes of Olynthus, great nephew to Aristotle. Both Nichomachus and Phaestis died when Aristotle was about ten years old, and Aristotle became the ward of Proxenus of Atarneus. Proxenus taught him Greek, rhetoric, and poetry, thereby complementing the biological education that Nicomachus had given him.

In 367, at the age of seventeen, Aristotle went to Athens to study at Plato's Academy, which had by then already become a pre-eminent centre of learning. While Plato and Aristotle certainly had differences of opinion, there was no lack of cordial appreciation or of that mutual forbearance which might be expected from men of lofty character. Aristotle remained at the Academy for nearly twenty years and left around the time of Plato's death in 347. The reasons for his departure are unclear: he may have felt slighted that the scholarchship (or leadership) of the Academy had passed on to Plato's nephew Speusippus, or he may have been opposed to Speusippus' views, or he may have left before Plato's death for fear of growing anti-Macedonian feelings.

Then in his thirty-seventh year, Aristotle travelled with Xenocrates of Chalcedon to Assos on the north-western coast of Asia Minor (modern day Turkey) to join the court of his friend Hermias of Atarneus. He may or may not have travelled to Assos as an ambassador for Philip. In either case, it seems that he exerted a moderating influence on Hermias, who softened his harsh tyrannical rule and introduced reforms consistent with Platonic principles of government. Aristotle married Hermias' niece and adoptive daughter, Pythias, who was then probably around eighteen years old, and Pythias bore him a daughter, also called Pythias. In 344, Hermias was captured by the Persians and tortured for information about Philip's plans, but Hermias kept his silence. His dying words were that he had done nothing shameful or unworthy of philosophy, and Aristotle honoured him by dedicating a statue in Delphi and composing a hymn to Virtue. At around this time, Aristotle travelled with his pupil Theophrastus ('Divinely speaking' – the nickname given to him by Aristotle) to the nearby island of Lesbos where he researched the zoology of the island and Theophastrus its botany.

Some two years later Aristotle was invited by Philip to tutor his son Alexander, who was then thirteen years old. At the temple of the Nymphs near Mieza near the Macedonian capital of Pella, Aristotle gave lessons not only to Alexander, but also to two other future rulers, Ptolemy and Cassander. He probably had considerable influence over Alexander, who on his eastern conquests took with him a crowd of zoologists, botanists, and other researchers. It is said that Aristotle prepared for Alexander a special edition of Homer's *Iliad*, which inspired the young prince to model his life on that of the greatest of the Greek heroes of the Trojan War, the semi-divine Achilles. According to Plutarch and to Aulius Gellius, upon hearing that Aristotle had published some of his oral teachings, Alexander wrote to him from Asia,

> *Alexander to Aristotle, greeting. You have not done well to publish your books of oral doctrine; for what is there now that we excel others in, if those things which we have been particularly instructed in be laid open to all? For my part, I assure you, I had rather excel others in the knowledge of what is excellent, than in the extent of my power and dominion. Farewell.*

In 339, Xenocrates succeeded Speusippus as Scholarch of the Academy, with Aristotle being passed over for the scholarchship for a second time. By 335, Aristotle had returned to Athens where he established his own school in a public exercise area dedicated to the god Apollo Lykeois, whence its name, the *Lyceum*. Aristotle often discussed philosophical problems while walking along the shaded walks (*peripatoi*) of the *Lyceum*, for which reason affiliates of the school came to be known as 'peripatetics'. The *Lyceum* survived until 86, when Athens was sacked by the Roman general Lucius Cornelius Sulla Felix (Sulla being the only man in history to have attacked and occupied both Athens and Rome). Aristotle taught at the Lyceum for some twelve years, during which time he also wrote many of his works and collected the first great library of the Ancient World. After the death of his wife Pythias, he became involved with (but did not marry) Herpyllis of Stageira, who bore him a son whom he named after his father, Nicomachus. According to the Suda, he also kept an *eromenos* (younger male lover), the historian Palaephatus of Abydus.

Near the end of his life, Alexander ordered the execution as a traitor of Aristotle's grandnephew Callisthenes and this and other things soured the relationship between the king and his master. After Alexander's death in Babylon in 323, anti-Macedonian feelings in Athens flared up, and Eurydemon the hierophant denounced Aristotle for not holding the gods in honour. Aristotle fled to his country house at Chalcis on Euboea, an island off the Attic coast and the homeland of his mother's family. Referring to the trial and execution of Socrates in 399, he famously explained, 'I will not allow the Athenians to sin twice against philosophy'. He died of an abdominal complaint within the year on March 7 of 322, aged sixty-two. There is a story according to which he threw himself into the sea 'because he could not explain the tides', but this is unlikely to be true, as are other fanciful conjectures about his death. After Aristotle had left Athens, Theophrastus – who was not Macedonian but Lesbian – had stayed behind as *scholarch* of the peripatetic school, and in his will Aristotle made provisions for him and for others to take over the care of his children and of Herpyllis. He also left him his works and his library, and designated him as his successor at the *Lyceum*.

II. Corpus Aristotelicum

According to legend, while the infant Plato was sleeping in a bower of myrtles on Mount Hymettus, bees settled upon his lips, auguring the honeyed words that would one day flow through his mouth. In his *Lives of Philosophers*, Diogenes Laertes says that, in the night before Plato was introduced to him as a pupil, Socrates 'in a dream saw a swan on his knees, which all at once put forth plumage, and flew away after uttering a loud sweet note.' Cicero, who was himself one of the greatest stylists in antiquity, lauded Plato's subtle and mellifluous dialogues, but then added that, if Plato's prose was silver, that of Aristotle was 'a flowing river of gold'. This may come as a surprise to modern readers of Aristotle, whose treatises often seem badly organised, poorly written, and heavily technical – and yet it is difficult to doubt the judgement of a man like Cicero. One can only assume that Cicero had before him works that have since been lost, such as the dialogues that Aristotle is known to have written earlier on in his career, probably while still at the Academy. The few fragments of these dialogues that remain suggest that they were written in a style similar to that of the Son of Apollo, who was then Aristotle's master.

While the lost works of Aristotle appear to have been intended for publication, this is not the case for the surviving works, the so-called *Corpus Aristotelicum*, which are not dialogues but technical philosophical treatises from within Aristotle's school. They were probably lecture notes or student texts, and were almost certainly repeatedly reworked over a period of several years. Although their prose is unembellished, this does not usually detract from their philosophical content, and some scholars even come to admire them for their candour and clarity. Aristotle divided his writings into two groups, those intended for the public ('exoteric') and those intended for his students and for other specialists ('esoteric'), and it is possible that all of his extant writings are from the second, esoteric group. According to Strabo and to Plutarch, Aristotle willed his esoteric writings to Theophrastus, who in turn willed them to his student Neleus of Scepsis, who supposedly took them from Athens to Scepsis. Neleus's heirs hid them in a vault, where they were discovered by the famous book collector Apellicon of Teos some two hundred years later, in the first century BC. According to the story, Apellicon repatriated the dilapidated manuscripts to Athens, wherefrom Sulla, who occupied Athens in 86 BC, removed them to Rome. They were then edited and published by the peripatetic philosopher Andronicus of Rhodes.

The works in the *Corpus Aristotelicum* can be classified into one of several groups according to their subject matter. Aristotle referred to the branches of learning as 'sciences', which he divided into three groups: theoretical sciences, practical sciences, and productive sciences. Theoretical sciences are concerned with knowledge for the sake of knowledge, and comprise both natural sciences and non-empirical forms of knowledge such as mathematics and 'first philosophy' (metaphysics). Practical sciences are concerned with good conduct and action both at the individual level, as in ethics, and at the societal level, as in politics. Productive sciences are concerned with the creation of beautiful or useful artefacts, and include, among many others, agriculture, medicine, music, and rhetoric. Logic, that is, the branch of learning that is concerned with the principles of intellectual inquiry, does not fit into this tripartite division of the sciences, but stands apart under the heading of *Organon* or 'Tool'.

Not all the works in the *Corpus Aristotelicum* are considered to be genuine, and the list that follows is composed only of those that are. The works are referred to by their English titles, but their Latin titles and standard abbreviations, which are often used by scholars, are also given. The works are ordered by their Bekker numbers, which are named after the classical philologist August Immanuel Bekker, editor of the Prussian Academy of Sciences edition in Greek of the complete works of Aristotle (1831–1870). The Bekker numbers are based on the page numbers used in the Bekker edition, and take the format of up to four digits, a letter for column 'a' or 'b', and then the line number. For example, the beginning of *On the Soul* is 402a1, which corresponds to the first line of the first column on page 402 of the Bekker edition. Bekker numbers are included in all modern editions or translations of Aristotle that are intended for scholarly readers, and enable citations to be cross-checked in any edition or translation that contains the numbers. The equivalent numbering system for the *Corpus Platonicum* is the Stephanus pagination.

Organon

Categories [*Categorie*, Cat.]
On Interpretation [*De Interpretatione*, DI]
Prior Analytics [*Analytica Priora*, APr]
Posterior Analytics [*Analytica Posteriora*, APo]
Topics [*Topica*, Top.]
Sophistical Refutations [*De Sophisticis Elenchis*, SE]

Theoretical Sciences

Physics [*Physica*, Phys.]
On the Heavens [*De Caelo*, DC]
Generation and Corruption [*De Generatione et Corruptione*, Gen. et Corr.]
Meteorology [*Meteorologica*, Meteor.]
On the Soul [*De Anima*, DA]

Brief Natural Treatises [*Parva Naturalia*, PN]
    Sense and Sensibilia
    On Memory
    On Sleep
    On Dreams
    On Divination in Sleep
    On Length and Shortness of Life
    On Youth, Old Age, Life and Death, and Respiration
History of Animals [*Historia animalium*, HA]
Parts of Animals [*De Partibus Animalium*, PA]
Movement of Animals [*De Motu Animalium*, MA]
Progression of Animals [*De Incessu Animalium*, LA]
Generation of Animals [*De Generatione Animalium*, GA]
Metaphysics [*Metaphysica*, Met.]

Practical Sciences

Nicomachean Ethics [*Ethica Nicomachea*, EN]
Eudemian Ethics [*Ethica Eudemia*, EE]
Politics [*Politica*, Pol.]

Productive Sciences

    Rhetoric [*Ars Rhetorica*, Rhet.]
    Poetics [*Ars Poetica*, Poet.]

III. Influence

Live and die in Aristotle's works.

– Christopher Marlowe, *Faust*

After Sulla removed Aristotle's esoteric writings to Rome, they were edited and published by the peripatetic philosopher Andronicus of Rhodes. By late antiquity they had almost fallen out of circulation, hampered by the rise of the Church and of neo-Platonism, the fall of Rome, and the loss of the Greek language among educated people. In the early sixth century, the Christian philosopher Boethius translated Aristotle's works on logic into Latin, and, for centuries to come, these were the only significant portions of Aristotle's writings (and indeed of Greek philosophy) available in the Occident. However, the study of Aristotle continued unabated in the Orient, in the Byzantine Empire and more particularly in the Abbasid Caliphate, where Persian and Arab philosophers such as Al-Farabi, Avicenna, and Averroes wrote extensive commentaries on Aristotle, whom they referred to deferentially as The First Teacher.

In the twelfth century, this Aristotelian fervour spilt over into Christian Europe. In the Condemnations of 1210–1277, the Bishops of Paris prohibited Aristotle's physical writings on the grounds of heterodoxy, but without much success. In the thirteenth century William of Moerbeke produced a Latin translation of Aristotle's writings from the original Greek text rather than from Arabic translations, the first complete Latin translation faithful both to the spirit and to the letter of Aristotle. At around the same time, Albert the Great and his preeminent student Thomas Aquinas, the *Doctor Angelus*, sought to reconcile Christian thought with Aristotle, whom they and other scholastic thinkers spoke of simply as The Philosopher. Under the aegis of the Church, Aristotelian ideas achieved such prominence and such propriety as to be assimilated to God-given gospel, only to be overturned centuries later by pioneers like Galileo, Descartes, and Newton.

Despite his prejudices against women, slaves, and non-Greek foreigners ('barbarians'), Aristotle is without a doubt one of the greatest philosophers of all time, and, along with Plato, one of the most influential people in Western history. Raphael's Renaissance masterpiece *The School of Athens* depicts Plato and Aristotle walking side by side, surrounded by a number of other philosophers and personalities of antiquity. An elderly Plato is holding a copy of his *Timaeus* and pointing vertically to the lofty vault above their heads, while a younger Aristotle is holding a copy of the *Nicomachean Ethics* and gesturing horizontally towards the descending steps at their feet. Plato was chiefly interested in moral philosophy, and held natural philosophy, that is, science, to be an inferior and unworthy type of knowledge. His idealism culminated in the Theory of the Forms, according to which knowledge of the truth cannot be acquired through the sense experience of imperfect particulars, but only through the rational contemplation of their universal essences or Forms. Aristotle flatly rejected the Theory of the Forms and emphasised that all philosophy should be grounded in the simple observation of particulars. In so doing, he laid the foundations for the scientific method, and his meticulous zoological observations remained unsurpassed for centuries to come. His moral philosophy prevailed throughout the ancient and mediaeval periods, exerting a profound influence on Christian thought, and returned to due prominence in the twentieth century with the resurgence of virtue ethics. His extant works, to say nothing of those that have been lost, cover such a wide range of topics, from aesthetics to astronomy and from politics to psychology, as to constitute a quasi encyclopaedia of Greek knowledge. Some of his most important works are *Physics*, *Metaphysics*, *Nicomachean Ethics*, *Politics*, *On the Soul*, *Poetics*, and, of course, the *Organon*, with which he created the field of logic and dominated it so thoroughly and for so long that even Kant in the eighteenth century thought that he had said the last word upon it.

More than any other figure in Western history, Aristotle is the embodiment of knowledge and of learning. His ideas have shaped centuries of thought and are still keenly pored over by all those who seek to understand the Western worldview, or simply to inhabit one of the greatest minds and systems of all time.

SECTION 2 –
ARISTOTLE'S WORKS

CHAPTER 1

Nicomachean Ethics

One swallow does not make a summer, nor does one day; and so too one day, or a short time, does not make a man blessed and happy.

Book 1

For Aristotle, a thing is best understood by looking at its end, goal, or purpose (*telos*). For instance, the end of a knife is to cut, and it is by grasping this that one best understands what a knife is; the end of medicine is good health, and it is by grasping this that one best understands what medicine is (or ideally should be). If one does this for some time, it soon becomes apparent that some ends are subordinate to higher ends, which are themselves subordinate to still higher ends.

> *If, then, there is some end of the things we do, which we desire for its own sake (everything else being desired for the sake of this) ... clearly this must be the good and the chief good. Will not the knowledge of it, then, have a great influence on life? Shall we not, like archers who have a mark to aim at, be more likely to hit upon what is right?*[1]

1   Translated by WD Ross.

The science that has for object the chief good, and whose end therefore includes that of all the others, is none other than the political art. To obtain the chief good for one person is fine enough, but to obtain it for the state is finer and more godlike. In inquiring into the chief good, care must be taken not to be too precise: fine and just actions admit of much variety and fluctuation of opinion, and 'it is the mark of an educated man to look for precision in each class of things just so far as the nature of the subject admits'.

People agree that the chief good is happiness (*eudaimonia*), but the many and the wise disagree as to its nature. The many and vulgar identify happiness with sensual pleasure, but a life of sensual pleasure is no better than that of a beast. People of superior refinement and active disposition identify happiness with honour, but honour is merely a mark of virtue, and, moreover, one that is reliant upon the recognition of others. Neither can happiness be identified with virtue itself, for then happiness would be compatible with a lifetime of sleep or inactivity or with the greatest sufferings and misfortunes.

According to Plato there is such a thing as the Form of the Good in which all good things share. However, this notion should be rejected as 'piety requires us to honour truth above our friends'. Aristotle raises eight objections to the Theory of the Forms, but claims that this is not the place to investigate it. He revisits the subject in the *Metaphysics*.

Returning to the search for the chief good, a goal that is an end in itself is more worthy of pursuit than one that is merely a means to an end, and a goal that is never a means to an end but only ever an end in itself is more worthy of pursuit than one that is or can be both.

> *Now such a thing happiness, above all else, is held*
> *to be; for this we choose always for self and never*
> *for the sake of something else, but honour, pleasure,*
> *reason, and every virtue we choose indeed for*
> *themselves (for if nothing resulted from them we*

should still choose each of them), but we choose
them also for the sake of happiness, judging that
by means of them we shall be happy. Happiness,
on the other hand, no one chooses for the sake of
these, nor, in general, for anything other than itself.

All well and good, but what does happiness actually consist
in? It is by understanding the distinctive function of a thing
that one can understand its essence. For instance, one cannot
understand what it is to be a gardener unless one can understand
that the distinctive function of a gardener is 'to tend to a garden
with a certain degree of skill'. Whereas human beings need
nourishment like plants and have sentience like animals, their
distinctive function is their unique capacity to reason. Thus the
Supreme Good, or Happiness, for human beings is to lead a life
that encourages the exercise and development of reason and
the practice of virtue. Happiness resides not so much in the
possession as in the practice *(energeia)* of reason and virtue, for
just as it is not the strong and beautiful but those who compete
well who win at the Olympic Games, so it is not the wise and
virtuous but those who act well who win – and rightly win – the
noble and good things in life. Their life is also more pleasant,
as virtuous actions are pleasant by nature, and all the more
pleasant still to the lover of virtue.

Now for most men their pleasures are in conflict
with one another because these are not by nature
pleasant, but the lovers of what is noble find
pleasant the things that are by nature pleasant;
and virtuous actions are such, so that these are
pleasant for such men as well as in their own
nature. Their life, therefore, has no further need of
pleasure as a sort of adventitious charm, but has
its pleasure in itself.

A person's good or bad fortune can play a part in
determining his happiness; for instance, happiness can be

affected by such factors as material circumstances, social position, and even physical appearance. Yet, by living life to the full according to his essential nature as a rational being, a person is bound to become happy regardless of his good or bad fortune. For this reason, happiness is more a question of behaviour and of habit – of excellence and of virtue – than of luck. A person who cultivates reason and who lives according to rational principles is able to bear his misfortunes with equanimity, and thus can never be said to be truly unhappy. Even the greatest misfortunes can be borne with resignation, not through insensibility to pain but through nobility and greatness of soul.

With regards to the soul, it comprises a rational and an irrational part. The irrational part has a vegetative element that is concerned with nutrition and growth, and an appetitive element that contains a person's impulses and that more or less obeys the rational part. If the rational part is strong, as in the virtuous person, it is able to exert a greater degree of control over the appetitive element of the irrational part. Similarly, there are two kinds of virtue, one that pertains to the intellect and that consists in philosophic and practical wisdom (intellectual or dianoetic virtues), and another that pertains to the character and that consists in liberality and temperance (moral or ethical virtues). A person may be praised for either or both kinds of virtue.

Book 2

Intellectual virtues are developed through teaching, and moral virtues through habit. Moral virtues are not in our nature, but nor are they contrary to our nature, which is adapted to receive them. Sight and hearing are in our nature, and so they are given to us. In contrast, the arts and the moral virtues are not given to us, but are acquired through constant exercise. Just as a man becomes a sculptor by sculpting, so he becomes just by doing just acts, temperate by doing temperate acts, brave by doing brave acts.

It is impossible to define virtue with any precision, as the goodness of a feeling or action depends on individual circumstances. However, just as strength is destroyed by a defect or excess of exercise, so the virtues are destroyed by their defect or excess. For instance, he who flies from everything becomes a coward, whereas he who meets with every danger becomes rash. In contrast, courage is preserved by the mean.

Moral excellence is closely related to pleasure and pain: it is in pursuing and avoiding pleasure and pain that bad things are done and noble things not, and so it is by pleasure and pain that bad people are bad. There are three objects of choice, the noble, the advantageous, and the pleasant, and three objects of avoidance which are their contraries, the base, the injurious, and the painful. The good tend to go right, the bad wrong, about these, and especially about pleasure which is common to the animals and which is also found in the advantageous and in the noble. A good person feels pleasure at the most beautiful or noble (*kalos*) actions, whereas a person who is not good often finds his perceptions of what is most pleasant to be misleading. It is harder to fight with pleasure than with anger, but both art and virtue are concerned with what is harder, and even the good is better when it is harder.

A person may do a seemingly virtuous action by chance or under compulsion. His action is truly virtuous only if (1) he knows that the action is virtuous, (2) he chooses to do the action for the sake of being virtuous, (3) his action proceeds from a firm and unchangeable character. In short, an action is truly virtuous if it is such as a virtuous person would do.

> *But most people do not do these, but take refuge in theory and think they are being philosophers and will become good in this way, behaving somewhat like patients who listen attentively to their doctors, but do none of the things they are ordered to do.*

There are three things that are found in the soul, passions, faculties, and dispositions (*hexeis*). As the virtues are neither passions nor faculties, they must be dispositions. In light of this, virtue can be defined as a disposition to aim at the intermediate between deficiency and excess, or, in other words, as a disposition to aim at the mean, which, unlike deficiency or excess, is a form of success and worthy of praise. While it is possible to fail in many ways, it is possible to succeed in one way only, which is why the one is easy and the other is difficult. By the same token, men may be bad in many ways, but good in one way only.

So far so good, except that not every passion or action admits of a mean, for instance, not envy or murder. It is never a question of murdering the right person, at the right time, and in the right way, for murder is bad in itself and neither a deficiency nor an excess. The principle virtues along with their corresponding vices are listed in Table 1.

Table 1: The principal virtues and vices			
Sphere of feeling or action	**Excess (vice)**	**Mean (virtue)**	**Deficiency (vice)**
Fear and confidence	Rashness	Courage	Cowardice
Pleasures and pains	Self-indulgence	Temperance	Insensibility (rare)
Getting and spending (minor)	Prodigality	Liberality	Meanness
Getting and spending (major)	Tastelessness	Magnificence	Niggardliness
Honour and dishonour (major)	Vanity	Proper pride	Pusillanimity
Honour and dishonour (minor)	Ambition	Proper ambition	Lack of ambition
Anger	Irascibility	Good temper	Lack of spirit
Self-expression	Boastfulness	Truthfulness	Mock modesty
Conversation	Buffoonery	Wittiness	Boorishness
Disposition to others	Obsequiousness	Friendliness	Cantankerousness
Shame	Bashfulness	Modesty	Shamelessness
Indignation	Envy	Proper indignation	Spite

In some cases, one vice can be closer to the virtue than the contrary vice, for instance, rashness is closer to courage than cowardice, and prodigality is closer to liberality than meanness. This is not only because the first vice is more similar to the virtue than the contrary vice, but also because the contrary vice is the more common. Rashness is more similar to courage than cowardice, which is more common than rashness, and prodigality is more similar to liberality than meanness, which is more common than prodigality. Hence people oppose not rashness but cowardice to courage, and not prodigality but meanness to liberality.

It is no easy task to be good. For a person to increase his likelihood of hitting the mean, he should (1) avoid the vice that is furthest from the virtue, (2) consider his vices and drag himself to their contrary extremes, (3) be wary of pleasure which clouds judgement and leads astray. The person may miss the mean by a little, for instance, he may get angry too soon or not enough, and still be praised for being either manly or good-tempered. It is only if he deviates more widely from the mean that he becomes blameworthy; how widely is difficult to determine, as it depends on the individual circumstances and on how they are perceived.

> *For in everything it is no easy task to find the middle ... anyone can get angry – that is easy – or give or spend money; but to do this to the right person, to the right extent, at the right time, with the right motive, and in the right way, that is not for everyone, nor is it easy; wherefore goodness is both rare and laudable and noble.*

Book 3

Actions are either voluntary, in which case they attract praise or blame, or involuntary, in which case they are forgiven (and sometimes also pitied). An action is involuntary if it takes place out of ignorance or if it takes place under compulsion, that is, if it originates from outside the person. An action that originates from inside a person who is under threat is in a grey area, but is more alike to a voluntary action than to an involuntary action.

> *For such actions men are sometimes even praised, when they endure something base or painful in return for great and noble objects gained; in the opposite case they are blamed, since to endure the greatest indignities for no noble end of for a trifling end is the mark of an inferior person.*

The term 'involuntary' should only be used for ignorance of particulars and not for ignorance of universals, since it is through ignorance of universals that people are made bad. For instance, a person who reveals a secret because he did not know it to be a secret is acting involuntarily, whereas a person who reveals a secret because he is ignorant of what he ought and ought not to do is acting non-voluntarily. The former repents his action, but the latter does not.

It is choices more than voluntary actions that reveal character, for even children and animals share in voluntary actions if they are done on the spur of the moment out of appetite or anger. Choices, which relate to means, are not the same as wishes, which relate to ends, including ends that are outside our power or that are impossible. Neither are choices the same as opinions, which are distinguished not by badness or goodness but by falsity or truth. It is not through our opinions that our character can be determined, but through our choices, and the people who have the best opinions and the people who make the best choices are not one and the same.

Choices imply deliberation, and deliberation is about the means that are in our control to achieve an outcome that is wished for. In deliberating and choosing the means, the good wish for the good, whereas the not good may understand things incorrectly and wish only for the apparent good, which is vice. Thus, both virtue and vice are voluntary, which is why people are honoured for their virtuous acts and punished for their vicious ones (unless done out of ignorance or under compulsion). Indeed, people are punished for their very ignorance, as when penalties are doubled in the case of drunkenness. Just as they are held responsible for their ignorance, so they should be held responsible for their bad character.

> *We may suppose a case in which [a man] is ill voluntarily, through living incontinently and disobeying his doctors. In that case it was then open to him not to be ill, but not now, when he has thrown away his chance ... So, too, to the unjust and to the self-indulgent man it was open at the beginning not to become men of this kind, and so they are unjust and self-indulgent voluntarily; but now that they have become so it is not possible for them not to be so.*

Turning from the general to the particular, courage is a mean with respect to things that inspire fear and confidence. Courage is not synonymous with fearlessness, since there are some evils such as disgrace or envy that even a brave person should fear. Instead, it involves confidence in the face of terrible things, and the most terrible of all things is death. A deficiency of fearfulness is rashness, whereas an excess is cowardice. The coward is a despairing sort of person as he fears everything. The brave person, on the other hand, has the opposite disposition, for confidence is the mark of a hopeful disposition. Those who may appear to be brave without actually being brave include those who act to gain honour or to avoid disgrace or punishment, those who act from habit or experience, those who act from passion, those who act because they are apt to prevail, and those who act without knowledge of the danger. Courage is particularly deserving of praise because it is harder to face what is painful than to abstain from what is pleasant, even though the end of courage is pleasant.

Temperance is a mean with respect to bodily pleasures, and more specifically to those bodily pleasures that the other animals share in, namely, those related to food and drink and sexual intercourse. As these attach to us not as men but as animals, to delight in them and to love them above all others is base and brutish. A deficiency of temperance is self-indulgence, and an excess – which is rare – is insensibility. The self-indulgent person not only prioritises what is pleasant, but is pained by its absence or by his abstinence from it. In contrast, the temperate person desires moderately and as he should the pleasant things that make for health and fitness or that do not detract from them, and that are neither base nor beyond his means. Self-indulgence is more voluntary than cowardice because it involves a pleasure to be chosen rather than a pain to be avoided.

Book 4

Liberality is a mean with respect to the taking and, above all, to the giving of all things whose value is measured by money. A deficiency of liberality is meanness, and the corresponding excess is prodigality. As the liberal is useful, he is almost the most loved of all virtuous characters. The liberal gives for the sake of the noble, with pleasure and without pain, to the right people, the right amounts, at the right time, and in the right way. Liberality resides not in many gifts but in the character of the giver, such that a person who gives less might well be the more liberal. Turning to the vices, meanness is more common than prodigality, and has many forms. A prodigal person is better than a mean one, for though he is foolish he is not wicked, and his vice is easily cured both by age and by poverty. Unfortunately, most prodigal people feel the need to take from the wrong sources, and in this respect they are also mean. Magnificence is liberality on a grand scale, except that it does not extend to all actions that are concerned with wealth, but only to those that involve expenditure. The magnificent person is like an artist in that he can see what is fitting and spend large sums tastefully. He spends not on himself but on public objects, and his gifts bear some resemblance to votive offerings. A deficiency of magnificence is niggardliness, and an excess is tastelessness. Although these states of character are vices, yet they do not bring disgrace because they are neither particularly harmful nor particularly unseemly.

A person is proud if he both is and thinks himself to be worthy of great things. If he both is and thinks himself to be worthy of small things he is not proud but temperate, for pride implies greatness. In terms of the vices, a person who thinks himself worthy of great things when he is unworthy of them is vain, whereas a person who thinks himself worthy of less than he is worthy of is pusillanimous. Compared to vanity, pusillanimity is both commoner and worse, and so more opposed to pride. Although the proud person is an extreme in respect of the greatness of his claims, he is a mean in respect of their truthfulness. He is avid of his just deserts and particularly of honour which is the prize of virtue and the greatest of external goods. He is moderately pleased to accept great honours conferred by good people, but he utterly despises honours from casual people and on trifling grounds. As a person who deserves more is better, the truly proud person is good, and as he is good, he is also rare. In sum, pride is a crown of the virtues; it is not found without them, and it makes them greater. The proud person is liable to disdain and to despise, but as he thinks rightly, he does so justly, whereas the many disdain and despise at random. Although the proud person is dignified towards the great and the good, he is unassuming towards the middle classes; for it is a difficult and lofty thing to be superior to the former, but easy to be so to the latter. Moreover, a lofty bearing over the great and the good is no mark of ill-breeding, but among humble people it is as vulgar as a display of strength against the weak.

> *Again, it is characteristic of the proud man not*
> *to aim at the things commonly held in honour, or*
> *the things in which others excel; to be sluggish*
> *and to hold back except where great honour or*
> *a great work is at stake, and to be a man of few*
> *deeds, but of great and notable ones. He must also*
> *be open in his hate and in his love (for to conceal*
> *one's feelings, i.e. to care less for truth than for*
> *what people will think, is a coward's part), and*
> *must speak and act openly; for he is free of speech*
> *because he is contemptuous, and he is given to*
> *telling the truth, except when he speaks in irony*
> *to the vulgar.*

With smaller honours there is also a mean, proper ambition, an excess, ambition, and a deficiency, lack of ambition.

Good temper is a mean with respect to anger. Good temper is closer to its deficiency, lack of spirit, than to its excess, irascibility, which is commoner than lack of spirit. A good tempered person sometimes gets angry, but only as he ought to.

Aristotle next discusses the virtues of friendliness, truthfulness, and wittiness, along with their corresponding vices. Modesty, he says, is more a feeling than a virtue since a virtuous person never does anything shameful and so has no need for modesty. Modesty is appropriate only in the young, in whom an appropriate feeling of shame fosters virtue.

Book 5

The just is the fair and the lawful, the unjust the unfair and the unlawful. As the laws aim at the good, the just person, who by definition is lawful, is also virtuous. However, whereas virtue is properly concerned with our moral state, justice is properly concerned with our relations with others. For this reason, justice alone among the virtues is thought to be 'another's good'; the best person is not he who exercises his virtue towards himself, but he who exercises it towards others, which is the more difficult task.

Apart from this kind of universal justice that includes not only justice but also the other virtues, there is a particular justice that has to do with greed aimed at particular goods such as money or honour or security. Actions are unjust in the universal sense if they are concerned with some vice such as self-indulgence, cowardice, or anger, and in the particular sense if they are concerned with greed aimed at particular goods.

Particular justice can be divided into distributive justice and rectificatory justice. Distributive justice concerns the distribution of things such as money or honour, which are to be distributed according to individual merit such that equals in virtue are given equal shares. Rectificatory justice concerns the rectification by a judge of unjust transactions between one person and another such that gains and losses are equaled out, whether or not the persons are equals. Rectificatory justice can itself be divided into rectification of voluntary transactions such as sale, purchase, loan, and rectification of involuntary transactions. Involuntary transactions are either clandestine such as theft, adultery, poisoning, or violent such as assault, imprisonment, murder.

The just in distribution is a mean or proportion which is an intermediate between at least four terms, two persons and two things, with the ratio between one pair being the same as that between the other pair. In other terms, A is to B as C is to D, and so A is to C as B is to D. The just in distribution is a geometrical proportion, the unjust violates the geometrical proportion. In contrast to the just in distribution, the just in rectification is a sort of straight and simple equality, and the unjust a straight and simple inequality, according to not geometric but arithmetic proportion.

In contrast to distributive justice and rectificatory justice, reciprocal justice ('an eye for an eye') is, as the Pythagoreans said, without qualification. First, if an official inflicts a wound, he ought not to be wounded in return, but if someone has wounded an official, he ought not only to be wounded but to be punished in addition. Second, there is a great difference between a voluntary and an involuntary action. Reciprocal justice is not fit in associations for exchange such as the polis because it does not hold people together.

Political justice, which relies on rule of law, should be differentiated from domestic justice, which relies on respect. Thus, the justice of a master and the justice of a father are not the same as the justice of citizens (though they are like it), for there can be no injustice in the unqualified sense towards things that are one's own. Some people wrongly think that political justice relies entirely on legal convention, 'because that which is by nature is unchangeable and has everywhere the same force (as fire burns both here and in Persia), while they see change in the things recognized as just.' Instead, it relies partly on legal convention, which varies from one place to another, and partly on natural law, which is the same everywhere.

A person acts unjustly only if he acts voluntarily; if involuntarily, for instance, if in ignorance, he acts neither unjustly nor justly except in an incidental way. Mistakes made in ignorance and from ignorance are excusable, but those done in ignorance but not from ignorance, owing to some unnatural passion, are not excusable. To act justly is not easy, and to recognise the just from the unjust comes not so much from a knowledge of the laws as from a virtuous disposition. In some cases, the law may be inadequate, and equity may be required to produce justice. For this reason, equity is better than legal justice, although not better than absolute justice.

Book 6

One ought to choose neither the excess nor the defect but the intermediate, and the intermediate is determined by the dictates of the right rule, which it is incumbent upon us to explore. As aforementioned, the virtues of the soul can be divided into those of character (*ethos*), which have already been treated, and those of intellect (*dianoia*). The soul comprises an irrational and a rational part, and the rational part can be further divided into a contemplative part that is concerned with invariable truths, and a deliberative part that is concerned with the practical matters of human life. The good state of the contemplative part is truth, and that of the deliberative part is right choice, which is the efficient cause of action. Choice is deliberate desire, and cannot exist without a combination of intellect and character. Also, choice can only ever concern the future, for which reason Agathon is correct in saying,

> *For this alone is lacking even to God,*
> *To make undone things that have once been done.*

The types of disposition (*hexis*) by which the soul can arrive at truth are five in number: (1) scientific knowledge (*episteme*), which arrives at necessary and eternal truths through induction and syllogism; (2) art or technical skills (*techne*), which is a rational capacity to make; (3) practical wisdom (*phronesis*), which is a rational capacity to secure the good life and with which the political art is associated; (4) intuition (*nous*), which apprehends the first principles or unarticulated truths from which scientific knowledge is derived; (5) philosophic wisdom (*sophia*), which is scientific knowledge combined with intuition of the things that are highest by nature. Philosophic wisdom is the highest intellectual virtue, but practical wisdom is the intellectual virtue that is most closely connected to the deliberation and choice that are required for just action. Although it is through the moral virtues that a person does what is just, it is through the intellectual virtues that he knows what this is. The intellectual virtues are also ends in themselves, and therefore lead to happiness in their own right.

Book 7

There are three kinds of moral state to be avoided: vice, incontinence, brutishness. Their respective contraries are virtue, continence, and a heroic and divine kind of virtue. Both the godlike man and the brutish man are rarely to be found; the brutish man is found chiefly among barbarians, but some brutish qualities are also produced by disease or deformity. Much that is contradictory is popularly said about incontinence (*akrasia*). Do incontinent people act knowingly and, if so, in what sense? With what sorts of object are incontinent people concerned? How does incontinence differ from softness or effeminacy? The incontinent person is concerned not with any and every object, but with those with which the self-indulgent person is concerned. Whereas the self-indulgent person acts out of his own choice, this is not the case for the incontinent person. It is possible that the incontinent person has knowledge of right and wrong but fails to use this knowledge; or that he is in ignorance of the particular facts and acts on false premises; or that he is under the influence of passions, and in a condition similar to that of a person who is asleep, mad, or drunk; or that an appetite impels him to act hastily, without self-restraint or due consideration. Thus, Socrates appears to have been correct in arguing that all incontinence results from ignorance.

It is clear that the incontinent person is concerned with pleasures and pains. Of the things that produce pleasure, some, such as those concerned with the bodily pleasures of food and sex, are necessary, while others such as victory, honour, and wealth are worthy of choice in themselves but admit of excess. Going to excess with respect to the latter is incontinence, but only by reason of resemblance; although this type of excess should be avoided, it does not imply wickedness. Incontinence is closely related to self-indulgence, the difference being that a self-indulgent person acts out of choice whereas an incontinent person lacks such self-control. Incontinence out of anger is less disgraceful than incontinence out of appetite since anger accords to some extent with reason whereas appetite does not. Furthermore, anger is human and natural and therefore common, it does not involve guile or deception, and it is not accompanied by pleasure but by pain. As self-indulgence (*akolasia*) is a matter of choice, it is more disgraceful than incontinence; the self-indulgent person is unlikely to repent, and he who is less likely to repent is also less likely to be cured. Continence is preferable to endurance, since continence consists in conquering, whereas endurance consists merely in resisting. To continence is opposed incontinence, and to endurance is opposed softness or effeminacy, which is the inability to resist the pleasures or endure the pains that most other people can. Strong-headed resistance on the basis of a rational and even correct decision may resemble incontinence more than continence if it is simply a case of an opinionated, ignorant, or boorish person taking stubborn delight in his apparent victory. Continence differs from temperance in that it implies the presence of bad appetites, and in that it might also inhibit good appetites. Of the forms of incontinence, that of excitable people is more curable than that of those who deliberate but do not abide by their decisions, and those who are incontinent by habit are more curable than those who are incontinent by nature.

Some philosophers think that no pleasure is a good; others think that only some pleasures are good and that most are bad; and yet others think that all pleasures are good, even though they are not the supreme good. However, none of their many arguments is able to prove that pleasure is not a good or even the supreme good, this for three principle reasons. (1) The good or bad need not be simply good or bad, but good or bad for a certain person or at a certain time. (2) The good or bad is either an activity (*energeia*) or a state (*hexis*), and there are pleasures that come from being restored to our natural state, and pleasures – such as the pleasure of contemplation – that come from being in our natural state. (3) Pleasures are not processes but activities; as activities, they are also ends

33

in themselves. It is true that some pleasures are harmful, but this is only in a limited sense. On the other hand, the higher pleasures that are enjoyed by the temperate person are not harmful in any sense. If it can be agreed that pain is bad and to be avoided, then it can also be agreed that pleasure (the contrary of pain) is good and to be sought out. All men think that the happy life is pleasurable, and cannot conceive of an ideal of happiness that is divorced from pleasure. All animals avoid pain and pursue pleasure, and if some of the pleasures that they pursue are bad, this need not imply that all pleasures are bad or even that the supreme good is not some pleasure. Things that are pleasurable incidentally in that they act as restoratives are to be contrasted to things that are pleasurable by nature in that they stimulate the action of the healthy nature. These higher pleasures do not admit of pain and therefore neither of excess. If the majority of men prefer incidental pleasures to higher or natural pleasures, this is because of our vicious nature. In truth, pleasure is found more in rest than in movement, and God perpetually enjoys a single and unalloyed pleasure.

Books 8 & 9

> *After what we have said, a discussion of friendship would naturally follow, since it is a virtue or implies virtue, and is besides most necessary with a view to living. For without friends no one would choose to live, though he had all other goods; even rich men and those in possession of office and of dominating power are thought to need friends most of all; for what is the use of such prosperity without the opportunity of beneficence, which is exercised chiefly and in its most laudable form towards friends?*

Other than this, friendship protects prosperity, is a refuge in poverty and misfortune, keeps the young from error, assists the elderly, and stimulates to noble actions those in the prime of life. Friendship deepens thought and reinforces action. Parent feels it for offspring and offspring for parent, not only among men but also among most animals. It holds states together, and lawgivers care more for it than for justice. People who are friends have no need for justice, but people who are just need friendship as well, and the truest form of justice is a friendly quality. Friendship is not only necessary but noble, and it is those with the greatest virtue who are friends most of all. Some philosophers say that friendship is a kind of likeness, others say the opposite. But is there only one type of friendship?

This question may be cleared up by identifying the object of love. There are three grounds upon which a person might wish another well, who, to be truly a friend, must both recognise and reciprocate this well-wishing: that he is useful, that he is pleasant, or that he is good. These reasons differ from one another in kind, and it follows that so do the corresponding forms of love and friendship. Yet, only those who love each other because they are good love each other for themselves, whereas friendships that are founded on usefulness or pleasure are only incidental, and are easily dissolved if one or both parties ceases to be useful or pleasant. These break ups are made more difficult if one or both parties has misrepresented himself or has been misled into thinking that he is loved for himself rather than for some incidental attribute. After a break up, each party should retain some consideration for the other in honour of their former friendship. Friendships that are founded on usefulness are particularly frequent in the elderly, and those on pleasure in the young. As the young are both pleasure seeking and dominated by their emotions, they quickly fall in and out of love, changing often within a single day.

> *Perfect friendship is the friendship of men who are*
> *good, and alike in virtue; for these wish well alike to*
> *each other qua good, and they are good themselves.*
> *Now those who wish well to their friends for their*

> *sake are most truly friends; for they do this by*
> *reason of their own nature and not incidentally;*
> *therefore their friendship lasts as long as they are*
> *good – and goodness is an enduring thing.*

The good are not only good to each other, but also useful and pleasant, and this without qualification. It follows that love and friendship are to be found most and in their best form between such virtuous people. Unfortunately, such perfect friendships are as rare as virtuous people are, and require a lot of time and familiarity, for people cannot know and trust each other until, as the proverb says, they have eaten salt together. A wish for friendship may arise quickly, but perfect friendship itself does not, and then only in those who are loveable and who are conscious of this fact. In loving his friend, a person loves both the friend and that which is good for him personally, and this need not involve any contradiction. Thus, the person wishes the same things for himself and for his friend, and shares in the same joys and sorrows. He makes an equal return in goodwill and pleasantness, in accordance with the saying that friendship is equality.

There are some relationships, such as those between older and younger or ruler and subject, in which there is a clear inequality between the parties. In such unequal relationships, each party makes a different return according to the nature of the relationship. For instance, a father renders one thing to his son, and the son renders another, equally appropriate, thing to his father. At the same time, the son should love his father more than his father loves him, and in proportion to his superior merit – thereby re-establishing a sort of equality. If, however, persons are vastly unequal in virtue or in wealth or in anything else, then they cannot be friends, and men of no account do not expect to be friends with the best or wisest men.

Most people prefer to be loved rather than to love because they are avid of flattery. However, friendship depends more on loving than on being loved, and an enduring friendship requires due measures of loving. Like loves like, and this is especially true in the case of virtue, for virtuous people hold fast to each other, and neither go wrong nor let their friend go wrong. Wicked people on the other hand do not even remain like to themselves, let alone to each other, and become friends only for a short time so as to delight in each other's wickedness.

Just as friendship binds together individuals, so justice binds together communities. Friendship is closely related to justice, and the demands of justice increase with the strength of a friendship. For this reason, it is more terrible to defraud a friend than a citizen, more terrible not to help a brother than a stranger, and more terrible to wound a father than anyone else. At the same time, the friendship of kindred and that of citizens should be marked off from the rest on the grounds that they rely on a sort of compact and are therefore more like mere friendships of association.

There are three kinds of constitution, monarchy, aristocracy, and timocracy or polity, monarchy being the best kind and timocracy the worst. Their respective perversions are tyranny, oligarchy, and democracy, in which privileges are not extended according to merit and rulers look after their own interest rather than the common interest. Of the perversions, tyranny is the worst and democracy is the least bad, with the result that the perversion of the best is the worst and that of the worst is the best. The relationship between father and son is analogous to monarchy, that between man and wife to aristocracy, and that between brothers to timocracy. If these relationships become devoid of friendship or justice, they descend into the perversions of the constitutions to which they are analogous.

Complaints and reproaches tend to arise in the friendship of utility, since those who are friends on the ground of pleasure both get at the same time that which they desire, and those who are friends on the ground of virtue are anxious to do well by each other. Differences also tend to arise in friendships of superior and inferior, for each expects to get more out of the other, and the friendship ends up being dissolved. The better or more useful person expects that he should get more, or else he feels less like he is being a friend and more like he is performing an act of public service. The more needy or inferior person also thinks that he should get more, reasoning that else there is no use in being the friend of a good or powerful person. Each party is justified in his claim, and each should get more out of the friendship than the other – but not of the same thing. The superior person should get more honour, and the inferior person more gain. However, it is often the case that a benefactor loves his beneficiary more than his beneficiary loves him back because it is more pleasurable to give than to receive and because the benefactor is in some sense responsible for 'creating' the beneficiary, much like an artist creates a work of art. It is preferable to have a small number of meaningful friendships than many superficial ones. A virtuous person may be self-sufficient, yet he will seek out friends, for friendship is one of the greatest goods in life.

Book 10

In Book 10, Aristotle returns to the subject of pleasure, 'for it is thought to be most intimately connected with our human nature … and to enjoy the things we ought and to hate the things we ought has the greatest bearing on virtue of character.' Arguments must harmonise with the facts if they are to be believed, and if they are to stimulate those who understand them to live according to them. Eudoxus[2] thought that, since all things seek pleasure and avoid pain, pleasure must be the greatest good. Pleasure, he argued, is sought for its own sake and not for the sake of something else. Furthermore, it makes any good that it is added to more worthy of choice. However, this argument seems to show that it is merely one of the goods, and no more a good than any other, for every good is more worthy of choice along with another good than taken alone. It is by an argument of this kind that Plato proves that pleasure is not the greatest good.

2   A scholar and student of Plato.

Indeed, for Plato, the greatest good is wisdom, since the pleasant life is more desirable with wisdom than without, and wisdom cannot become more desirable by the addition of anything to it. No one would choose to live with the intellect of a child throughout his life, however pleasing that may be, nor to get enjoyment by doing the most disgraceful deeds, and there are many things that we should be keen about even if they brought no pleasure, for instance, seeing, remembering, knowing, and being virtuous. From this it is clear that (1) pleasure is not the greatest good, (2) not all pleasures are desirable, and (3) some pleasures are desirable in themselves.

Like sight, pleasure seems to be at any moment complete and the same in kind. For this reason, it is not a movement (e.g. that of building or walking), for any movement takes time and is for the sake of an end that is not the same in kind as the movements that lead to it.

> ...*while there is pleasure in respect of any sense, and in respect of thought and contemplation no less, the most complete is pleasantest, and that of a well-conditioned organ in relation to the worthiest of its objects is the most complete; and the pleasure completes the activity. But the pleasure does not complete it in the same way as the combination of object and sense, both good* [but] ... *as an end which supervenes as the bloom of youth does on those in the flower of their age.*

Pleasure is accompanied by activity, and it is because we are incapable of continuous activity that we are incapable of continuous pleasure. Upon being presented with something new, the mind is in a state of stimulation and intensely active, but then grows relaxed, for which reason the pleasure is also dulled. If we desire pleasure, it is because we aim at life, which is an activity. Those things which we are most active about are those which we love the most. Activity and pleasure are inextricably bound, and it is impossible to distinguish whether we choose life for the sake of pleasure or pleasure for the sake of life.

Activities differing in kind are completed by things also differing in kind, and so there are several kinds of pleasures. Since activities differ in respect of goodness and badness, so too do pleasures. Just as with activities, some pleasures are to be chosen, others are to be avoided, and yet others are neutral. Each animal is thought to have its proper pleasures, just as it has its proper functions; as Heraclitus says, 'asses prefer sweepings to gold'. Although it is plausible to suppose that the pleasures of a single species do not differ, in the case of man they vary to no small extent. The same thing does not seem sweet to a healthy man and a man in fever, but the perception of the healthy man is the most accurate. Similarly, with regard to the goodness and badness of pleasures and activities, the judgement of the virtuous man is the most accurate.

Having spoken of virtue, friendship, and pleasure, it remains to outline the nature of happiness, which is the end of human living. Happiness is not a disposition but an activity, for otherwise it might belong to someone who was asleep throughout his life, or to someone who was suffering the greatest misfortunes. Some activities are desirable for the sake of something else, while others are so in themselves, and it is among the latter that happiness must be placed, for happiness does not lack anything but is self-sufficient. Activities which are desirable in themselves are those from which nothing is sought beyond the activity, and of this nature virtuous actions are thought to be, and particularly so by the good or virtuous man. It would be strange if happiness lay in amusement rather than in virtuous actions, for then man would take trouble and suffer hardship all his life only to amuse himself. But to amuse oneself in order that one may exert oneself, as Anacharsis[3] puts it, seems right, for amusement is a sort of relaxation, necessary only because of the impossibility of continuous activity.

3   A Scythian philosopher of the 6th century BC who travelled to Athens.

And any chance person – even a slave – can enjoy
the bodily pleasures no less than the best man; but
no one assigns to a slave a share in happiness –
unless he assigns to him also a share in human
life. For happiness does not lie in such occupations,
but, as we have said before, in virtuous activities.

Of all the virtues, the virtue of contemplation leads to the greatest pleasure, for it is the best thing in man and also the most continuous. Philosophic wisdom is the most pleasant of all virtuous activities and gives rise to pleasures marvellous both for their purity and enduringness. Man more than anything is reason, and the life of reason is the most self-sufficient, the most pleasant, the happiest, the best, and the most divine of all. Indeed, the activity of God, which surpasses all others in blessedness, surely is contemplative; and of human activities, therefore, that which is most akin to this must be most of the nature of happiness. However, man is not self-sufficient for the purpose of contemplation, and also needs external prosperity, namely, health, food, and so on. Still, the man who is to be happy does not need many things or great things, and the life of virtue can be practiced, indeed, more easily practiced, with but moderate possessions. According to Anaxagoras, the happy man is bound to seem a strange person, since others can only perceive, and therefore judge by, externals.

Now if arguments were in themselves enough to
make men good, they would justly, as Theognis
says, have won very great rewards, and such
rewards should have been provided; but as things
are, while they seem to have power to encourage
and stimulate the generous-minded among our
youth, and to make a character which is gently
born, and a true lover of what is noble, ready to be
possessed by virtue, they are not able to encourage
the many to nobility and goodness.

41

Man is made good either by nature, or by habituation, or by teaching. Nature is not in our hands, and argument and teaching can only take hold in a soul that is noble or that has been cultivated by good habits, which themselves have arisen from good laws. Thus, he who wishes to make men better by his care must be capable of legislating well, and it is to the political art that I turn to next.

CHAPTER 2

Politics

Man is by nature a political animal.

Book 1

Every community aims at some good. The state or political community is the highest of all communities, and as such it aims at the highest good.

The origin of the state lies in a union of those who cannot exist without each other, of male and female, that the race may continue, and of natural ruler and subject, that both may be preserved. From this arises the family, then the village, and then the *polis* or state, which secures the highest self-sufficiency. From this it is evident that the state is a creation of nature, and that man is by nature a political animal. Man is the most political of all animals, more so even than the bees, for he alone has the gift of speech and the notion of good and evil. Moreover, the state is prior to the individual, for the whole is of necessity prior to the part, and the isolated individual is not self-sufficing. 'He who is unable to live in society, or who has no need because he is sufficient for himself, must be either a beast or a god: he is no part of the state.'[1] The first founder

1   Translated by Benjamin Jowett.

of the state was the greatest of benefactors, for man, when perfected, is the best of animals, but, when separated from law and justice, he is the worst of all.

The state is made up of households, which consist of the relations of master and slave, husband and wife, father and children. Another element of a household is the so-called art of getting wealth or property, of which slaves are a part. Some men are born for subjection and others for rule. Just as it is natural and expedient for the soul to rule over the body, or for reason to rule over the passions, or for men to rule over animals, so it is natural and expedient for masters to rule over slaves. Indeed, it is better for all inferiors that they should be under the rule of a master. However, it is unjust to enslave those who are not slaves by nature; if the relation of master and slave is natural then they are friends and have a common interest, but if it is only legal then the reverse is true. The rule of a household is a monarchy, for every house is under one head, whereas constitutional rule is a government of freemen and equals.

The art of managing a household is not the same as that of getting wealth, as the one uses the material which the other provides. However, natural acquisition – that is, the securing of food, shelter, and other necessities – is an indispensible part of the art of managing a household. Natural acquisition should not be confused with unnatural acquisition – that is, the accumulating of wealth for its own sake – which is not a part of the art of managing a household and which is as unlimited as it is unnecessary. The most hated sort of wealth getting is not retail but usury, for money is intended to be used in exchange, not to increase at interest. 'Enough has been said about the theory of wealth-getting ... the discussion of such matters is not unworthy of philosophy, but to be engaged in them practically is illiberal and irksome.'

Other than the rule of master over slaves, in the household there is also the rule of husband over wife and of father over children. A husband stands to his wife as a statesman to his people, whereas a father stands to his children as a king to his subjects. Unlike slaves, wife and children are free and possessed of the deliberative faculty, although in the woman the deliberative faculty is without authority and in the child it is immature. So it must be supposed to be with the moral virtues also. The courage of a man is in commanding, that of a woman in obeying, and this holds of all other virtues. As the poet says of women, 'Silence is a woman's glory.'

Book 2

Before expounding on his politics, Aristotle proposes to examine a number of theoretical and actual constitutions. He begins with Plato's *Republic*, which he criticises for advocating that citizens should have wives and children and property in common. Such a high degree of unity would lead to the destruction of the state, for the state is not made up only of so many people, but also of different kinds of people, and it is this plurality that secures its self-sufficiency. In any case, people do not care as much for the common interest as they do for their own self-interest. To hold all things in common runs against human nature, and would give rise to a number of social problems. For example, the friendship and love in family ties would be lacking, children would not receive proper parenting, and people would be more likely to quarrel with and assault one another. The entire class of guardians would be deprived of happiness, which cannot be said to exist in the whole unless it exists in the parts. Also lacking would be the pleasure that comes from doing a kindness or service to others, as the exercise of liberality depends on the existence of private property. 'Such legislation may have a specious appearance of benevolence; men readily listen to it, and are easily induced to believe that in some wonderful manner everybody will become everybody's friend ... Let us [then] not disregard the experience of ages; in the multitude of years these things, if they were good, would certainly not have been unknown; for almost everything has been found out...'

Aristotle turns to Plato's *Laws* and raises a number of similar objections. In the *Republic* the guardians number 1000 whereas in the *Laws* they number 5000. To support such a great number of people together with their women and attendants in idleness would require a territory as huge as Babylon. The legislator should look not only to the people and to the country, as Plato advocates, but also to neighbouring countries. 'Even if the life of action is not admitted to be the best, either for individuals or states, still a city should be formidable to enemies, whether invading or retreating.' The guiding principle regarding wealth should not be temperance alone, but temperance and liberality in combination, for temperance without liberality is associated with toil, and liberality without temperance with luxury and decadence. Population growth should be regulated if land is to be shared out equally. If not, supernumerary citizens will live in poverty, which is the parent of revolution and crime. Finally, whereas Plato intends the constitution in the *Laws* to be a polity, that is, a combination of several forms of government, he ends up with a quasi-oligarchy.

Aristotle examines two further theoretical constitutions, that of Phaleas of Chalcedon and that of Hippodamus of Miletus[2] By equalising land possessions, Phaleas may eliminate necessity and thereby petty crime, but the greatest crimes are not committed out of necessity. 'Men do not become tyrants in order that they may not suffer cold; and hence great honour is bestowed, not on him who kills a thief, but on him who kills a tyrant ... It is of the nature of desire not to be satisfied, and most men live only for gratification of it.'

2   Phaleas of Chalcedon was an ancient Greek statesman. Hippodamus of Miletus was an ancient Greek polymath who, under Perikles, designed the urban plan for Piraeus. He is still thought of as the father of urban planning.

Thus, it is not land possessions but desires that need to be equalised, and this can only be achieved through education. Furthermore, whereas equal land possessions would pacify the poor, it would incense the dispossessed rich, who would be sure to revolt. The state may also come under attack from the outside, for, like Plato, Phaleas looks only to the people and to the country, but not also to neighbouring countries. Hippodamus divided the 10000 citizens of his state into three parts, artisans, husbandmen, and warriors. The land also he divided into three parts, sacred land for worship, public land for the support of the warriors, and private land for the husbandmen. Aristotle raises various objections to the institutions of Hippodamus, in the course of which he says that laws should only be changed with great caution, and only if the advantage gained by doing so is significant. 'For the law has no power to command obedience except that of habit, which can only be given by time, so that a readiness to change from old to new laws enfeebles the power of the law.'

Having examined a number of theoretical constitutions, Aristotle turns his attention to actual constitutions, namely, those of Sparta (Lacedaemon), Crete, and Carthage. The Spartans constantly live under the threat of a revolt by their helots or husbandmen. Their constitution is largely silent about women, who are free to live in intemperance and luxury and to cultivate avarice and indolence. Land is unevenly distributed, and owing to dowries and inheritances, two-fifths of it is owned by women. As a result of this and of a reluctance to give citizenship to strangers, the number of Spartan citizens has fallen to fewer than 1000. In terms of government, the power of the five ephors is so great that even the two kings have been compelled to court them. As the ephors are chosen from the entire population, the ephoralty is liable to fall into the hands of very poor men who, being badly off, are open to bribes. Also open to bribes are members of the council of elders, who canvass for their office and, once elected, hold it for life. Instead, members of the council of elders should be chosen on the basis of their personal life and conduct, as should be the kings. Many citizens are so poor as to be unable to afford the *phiditia* or common meals, which are intended to be a popular institution and which should be publically funded. However, the Spartans are reluctant to pay taxes, the revenues of the state are poorly managed, and the treasury is empty. More fundamentally, the constitution has regard to one part of virtue only, namely, the virtue of the soldier. As a result, the Spartans know nothing of the arts of peace and have never engaged in any employment higher than war.

The Cretan constitution nearly resembles the Spartan, but is for the most part less perfect in form. The Cretan government may possess some of the characteristics of a constitutional state, but it is really a feuding oligarchy that survives only by virtue of the island's isolation from other states. The Carthaginian nearly resembles the Cretan and Spartan states, but it is so superior that the Carthaginians have never either suffered a rebellion or been under the rule of a tyrant. The Carthaginian government does tend to oligarchy, but escapes the evils of oligarchy by sending its citizens to be enriched in its colonies. This having been said, the legislator should be able to provide against revolution without trusting to accidents. Aristotle goes on, briefly, to discuss a number of historical legislators such as Solon and Philolaus of Corinth.

Book 3

Aristotle begins by defining the parts of a state, namely, the citizens. A citizen is not a citizen by virtue of living in a certain place or of having certain legal rights, or else resident aliens and slaves would also be citizens. Instead, a citizen is a citizen by virtue of having the power to take part in the deliberative or judicial administration of a state, which is a body of citizens sufficing for the purposes of life. In practice, however, a citizen is one of whom both the parents are citizens, but this definition cannot apply to the first citizens or founders of a state, nor to those who became citizens after a revolution or a change in the constitution. Questions arise as to whether all who are citizens ought to be citizens, and, if not, as to whether the state amounts to the government of its citizens. According to our definition of a citizen, anyone who participates in the government of the state is a citizen. However, the state does not amount to its citizenry, or indeed to its territory, but to its constitution. A change in constitution is tantamount to change in the state. The question also arises as to whether the virtue of a good citizen is the same as that of a good man. The virtue of the good citizen varies from one form of government to another, but the virtue of a good man is one and only. Therefore, it is possible for a man to be a good citizen but not a good man. Furthermore, the virtue of one citizen within a state is not necessarily the same as that of another, for citizens have different functions within the state. The virtue of the good citizen and the virtue of the good man might coincide, and the education of a ruler should be the same as that of a good and wise man. Lastly, the question arises as to whether those who do not share in an office, that is, the class of artisans, can be citizens. The best form of state should not admit them to its citizenship.

Aristotle next considers how many forms of constitution or government there are. First, a government may be just and regard the common interest, or unjust and regard only the interest of the rulers. Then, whether just or unjust, a government may be in the hands of one, a few, or the many (Table 2).

Table 2: Aristotle's six forms of government		
Rule of	**Just (in the common interest)**	**Unjust (in the interest of the rulers)**
One	Kingship or royalty	Tyranny
A few	Aristocracy	Oligarchy
The many	Constitutional government (rulers excel in military virtue only)	Democracy (rule is in the interest of the poor only)

If the end goal of the state is wealth, then the state should be apportioned according to property, as in an oligarchy. On the other hand, if the end goal of the state is life or security, then the state should be apportioned equally, as in a democracy. However, the end goal of the state is neither wealth nor life, but the good life; those who contribute the most to the good life should have a greater share in the state, regardless of their wealth or birth.

Whether the state is ruled by the poor, or the wealthy, or the good, or the one best man, or a tyrant, there appear to be disagreeable consequences. For example, if the poor divide among themselves the property of the rich, this is not only unjust but ruinous to the state.

> *Yet, surely, virtue is not the ruin of those who possess her, nor is justice destructive of the state; and therefore this law of confiscation cannot be just. If it were, all the acts of a tyrant must of necessity be just; for he coerces other men by superior power, just as the multitude coerce the rich.*

Rule by one man or by a few deprives the rest from the honour of holding public office. Furthermore, compared to the many, the one and the few are more vulnerable to all the accidents of human passion. Rule by the law may be preferable to rule by the one or by the few, but laws are only as good as those who wrote them. Constitutional government can overcome many of these difficulties. Taken collectively, the many often come to better decisions than the one or the few. Moreover, the many are better judges as to whether they are being well governed. While the many should not share singly in the great offices of state, they should share collectively in some deliberative and judicial functions. In conclusion, laws, when good, should rule supreme, and the governing bodies should only intervene in particular cases on which the law is silent or not well.

In all sciences and arts, the end is a good. The end of the political science is justice, and justice or the common interest is the greatest good. All men agree that justice is some sort of equality, but they disagree as to what. Wealth and freedom are necessary elements for holding office, but justice and valour are equally so; without the former qualities a state cannot exist at all, without the latter not well. Yet it is impossible to decide between these elements, and all states that rely on either one of them alone are perversions. Taken collectively, the many are often richer and better than the few. However, on rare occasions, there arises a person of such exceptional virtue as to outshine the political capacity of all the rest. Such a person is a god among men, and should be made king.

Kingship is one of the three just forms of government, but there are several kinds of kingship, ranging from perpetual military leadership to absolute monarchy. The law is reason unaffected by desire. Customary laws have more weight, and relate to more important matters, than written laws, and a man may be a safer ruler than the written law, but not a safer ruler than the customary law. When the law is silent or not well, it is better for many men to decide than for one man, so long as they are all of equal merit. The first governments were kingships because then cities were small and men of eminent virtue were few. When many persons equal in merit arose, they desired to have a commonwealth and set up a constitution.

The ruling class soon deteriorated and enriched themselves out of the public treasury. Riches became the path to honour, and so oligarchies sprang up. These passed into tyrannies and tyrannies into democracies.

Book 4

The best is often unattainable, and the true legislator and statesman ought to be acquainted not only with that which is best in theory, but also with that which is best in practice. Of the three just forms of government, kingship and aristocracy have already been discussed, and it remains only to discuss constitutional government – as well as the three unjust forms of government, tyranny, oligarchy, and democracy. Just as kingship can be the best of governments, so tyranny can be the worst of governments. Oligarchy is only a little better, leaving democracy as the best of a bad lot.

States vary greatly in terms of the wealth, merit, skills, and so on of their citizens, and accordingly there are many forms of government. However, there are only two principal forms of government, namely, democracy and oligarchy. Democracy is rule by the free, so long as the free are poor and in the majority. Oligarchy is rule by the rich, so long as the rich are few in number. In order to determine the different types of democracy and oligarchy, it is necessary to list the different parts of the state. These are nine in number: farmers, artisans and artists, merchants, serfs or labourers, warriors, wealthy patrons, and the executive, deliberative, and judicial branches of government. The parts of the state may overlap, for instance, a warrior may also be a farmer or an artisan, but the same cannot be said of the poor and the rich. If the poor, who are usually the many, are in power, this is democracy. If it is the rich, who are usually the few, this is oligarchy. There are five forms of democracy and four forms of oligarchy. The five forms of democracy are, that based strictly on equality, that in which the magistrates are elected according to a modest property qualification, that in which the law is supreme and all citizens share in government, that in which the law is supreme but only qualified citizens share in government, that in which not the law but the citizen body is supreme. This last form of democracy is a breeding ground for demagogues, and is to the other forms of democracy as tyranny is to the other forms of monarchy. It is also open to the objection that it is not a constitution at all, for where the laws have no authority, there is no constitution. The five forms of oligarchy are, that in which the property qualification for becoming a magistrate is high, that in which the property qualification for becoming a magistrate is high and magistrates are selectively co-opted, that in which the sons succeed the fathers and the law is supreme, that in which the sons succeed the fathers and they are supreme. This last is called a dynasty, and is to oligarchies as tyranny is to monarchies, and as the last form of democracy is to democracies. In a democracy, if the citizens have the leisure to share in the administration, then the state is governed by the many; if not, it is governed by the laws. In an oligarchy, if many citizens meet the qualification to share in the administration, then the state is governed by the laws; if not, it is governed by the few.

Aristocracy is, strictly speaking, participation on the basis of merit alone, and not on the basis of number or wealth. Polity or constitutional government is a fusion of democracy and oligarchy, although the term is generally applied to governments that incline towards democracy, and the term 'aristocracy' for those that incline towards oligarchy. A polity can be either a combination of democracy and oligarchy, a mean between the two, or a mixture of elements taken from each. The constitution of a polity should appear to have both elements and yet neither, and should be upheld by every class of citizen in the state.

Of tyrannies there are three kinds, that which is legal and hereditary and to be found among barbarians, that which is legal and elective and to be found in Greek states of old, and the most common kind which consists in the arbitrary power of an individual who governs for his own advantage and therefore against the will of the people.

The best constitution for most states, and the best life for most men, is the polity. If the happy life is the life of virtue lived without impediment, and if virtue is a mean,[3] then the life which is in a mean, and a mean attainable by everyone, must be the best. As the rich find it hard to obey, and as the poor find it hard to command, a city of the rich and poor is a city not of freemen but of masters and slaves, the one despising, the other envying. Good fellowship springs from friendship, and a city ought to be composed, as far as possible, of equals and similars, and these are generally the middle classes. Wisely did Phocylides pray, 'Many things are best in the mean; I desire to be of a middle condition in my city.' Compared to a city with a large middle class, a city of the rich and poor tends to pure oligarchy or to rampant democracy, and either extreme may degenerate into tyranny. Unfortunately, most states do not have a large middle class, and the middle form of government has rarely, if ever, existed, and then only among a very few.

Every state is composed of quality and quantity. If the quantity of the poor exceeds the quality of the rich, then a democracy is desirable. If, however, the quality of the rich and notables exceeds the quantity of the poor, then an oligarchy is desirable. The precise form of the democracy or oligarchy depends on the type of the quantity of the poor and on the type of the quality of the rich. In all cases, the legislator should include the middle classes in his government. The poor and the rich mistrust one another, and the role of the middle classes is to arbitrate between them.

In an oligarchy, the rich are compelled to participate in affairs of state or else they are fined. In a democracy, the poor are paid to participate, but the rich are neither paid to participate nor sanctioned for not participating. If all are to participate, the poor should be paid to participate, and the rich

3   See the *Nicomachean Ethics*.

fined for not participating. Although the poor should participate, participation should be limited to those who carry arms.

All constitutions have three elements, the deliberative, the executive, and the judicial. The deliberative element is the supreme element in a state: it enacts laws, determines foreign policy and matters of war and peace, inflicts severe punishments such as death and exile, and elects magistrates. The executive element commands and governs in the name of the deliberative element. The judicial element resolves disputes and punishes offences both in the public and the private spheres. In a polity, all citizens should participate in some functions, and only selected individuals in others. The nature of the executive element is determined by the number, type, and length of tenure of offices, and on the method of appointment to offices. Offices may be appointed by all or only some citizens, and from all or only some citizens, either by vote or by lot.

Book 5

Democracy arises out of the notion that those who are equal in freedom are also equal in all other respects, oligarchy out of the notion that those who are unequal in property are unequal in all other respects. Both parties stir up revolution whenever their share in the government does not accord with their preconceived ideas. Democracy and oligarchy are the two principal forms of government because numbers and wealth are common, whereas good birth and virtue are rare. Unfortunately, both are based on a mistake, and can never last, although democracy is safer and less liable to factionalism than oligarchy.

The causes of revolution include insolence and avarice among officials, desire of gain, desire of honour, over-concentration of power in a small number of officials, fear of being punished or of suffering wrong, contempt at poor government, a disproportionate increase in any part of the state, changes in electoral procedures, the careless selection and promotion of persons disloyal to the constitution, small constitutional changes adding up to major constitutional change, lack of social cohesion, quarrelling among notables, changes in the balance of power, equality of opposite parties, force, and deception or fraud.

In democracies, revolution is generally stirred up by unjust demagogues who wrong the notables and thereby compel them to join forces. In oligarchies revolution is stirred up if oligarchs oppress the people; oligarchs rival one another by playing the demagogue; oligarchs become impoverished and seek to raise funds; an oligarchy is created within the original one; after a period of prosperity, many people meet the property qualification for being an oligarch. An aristocracy is a sort of oligarchy, but with a different qualification for government. In aristocracies, revolution is stirred up if the governing class becomes overly exclusive or, as in polities, if the elements of democracy and oligarchy in the constitution become unbalanced. Revolution can also occur from the outside if another state seeks to impose its constitution on its neighbours, as Athens and Sparta have often sought to do.

The causes that preserve constitutions are the opposite of those that destroy them. To prevent revolution, governments should prevent lawlessness especially in small matters; avoid deceiving the masses; keep good relations with all segments of society and treat everyone fairly; create a state of alarm so as to keep the citizens on guard; prevent the notables from quarrelling with one another; adjust the qualification for government to changing times; avoid doling out or withdrawing great honours too quickly; prevent any part of the state or any one individual from having too much property or influence, and seek to add to that of the opposing class or of the middle class; prevent officials from making money out of government; look after the interests of the rich in a democracy, and of the poor in an oligarchy. The qualifications for occupying high office should be loyalty to the constitution, ability to govern, and virtue and justice of the kind proper to the prevalent form of government. Democracy and oligarchy are departures from the most perfect form of government, yet they may be good enough so long as they do not degenerate into extreme democracy or extreme oligarchy, which are effectively tyrannies in which power is distributed among several persons. The constitution should have the support of a majority and involve both the rich and the poor. Education should be adapted so that the young may be trained in the spirit of the constitution: it is in obedience to the constitution that men find their salvation.

With regard to monarchies, a kingship is of the nature of an aristocracy, and a tyranny is a compound of oligarchy and democracy in their most extreme forms, with all the errors and perversions of both. A king is usually a virtuous man taken from the notables by the notables and for the notables, whereas a tyrant is usually a demagogue taken from the people by the people and for the people. The king protects the rich against injustice and the people against insult and oppression, whereas the tyrant has no regard to any public interest except that which promotes his private ends. The king aims at honour, the tyrant at riches; the king is guarded by citizens, the tyrant by mercenaries. In monarchies as in constitutional governments, revolutions arise out of fear of, contempt for, or injustice on the part of sovereigns. Tyrannies may be destroyed from without by some opposite and more powerful form of government, or from within by the hatred and contempt of the people. Kingly rule, though increasingly rare, is longer lasting than tyranny, and is generally destroyed from within if the royals quarrel among themselves or if the king becomes a tyrant. A kingship is best preserved by limiting the powers of the king, a tyranny either by harsh repression or, conversely, by the tyrant masquerading as a king or steward. The most short-lived forms of government are oligarchy and tyranny. In the *Republic*, Plato does treat of the causes of revolutions, but not well.

Book 6

The mark of a democracy is freedom based upon equality. Democrats claim to be ruled by none, if possible, or, if this is impossible, to rule and be ruled in turn. Justice for a democrat is that to which the majority agree, for an oligarch, that to which the wealthy agree. However, in both principles there is some injustice: in a pure democracy, the poor may confiscate the property of the rich; in a pure oligarchy, a very rich person may install himself as tyrant.

The best material of democracy is an agricultural population, as farmers and herdsmen are too poor, too busy, and too rural to attend the assembly. Instead, they are happy to elect officials and call them to account. In this type of democracy, the great offices are filled up by election and from persons having a qualification or marked out by special ability. The poor are satisfied because they are governed with both accountability and skill, and the notables are satisfied because they are not governed by their inferiors. The worst material of democracy consists of mechanics, traders, and labourers, as these are far more likely to attend the assembly and thereby to promote mob rule and demagoguery.

To create a state is one thing, but to preserve it is quite another. The legislator should establish laws and customs that contain all the preservative elements of states, and guard against all the destructive ones. He should not be tempted by pure democracy or pure oligarchy, as both are inherently unstable. In a democracy, both the rich and the poor should be looked after. The rich should not have their property confiscated, and, if possible, the poor should be given the funds with which to buy a small farm or, at any rate, to make a beginning in trade or husbandry. In an oligarchy, there ought to be one standard of qualification for holding high office, and another, much more modest, one for holding minor offices. A country with strong cavalry or heavy infantry is better suited to an oligarchy, whereas a country with strong light infantry or naval forces is better suited to a democracy.

Every state needs a certain number of officers: magistrates to regulate commerce, maintain and develop the city's infrastructure, manage rural affairs, collect taxes, register private contracts and public rulings, and extract fines and carry out punishments. Equally necessary but of higher rank and requiring greater experience and loyalty are military commanders, accountants and controllers, councillors that preside over the public deliberations of the state, and priests and other religious guardians.

Book 7

Before determining the best form of state, it is necessary to determine the best form of life. Goods can be divided into three classes, external goods, goods of the body, and goods of the soul. Whereas goods of the soul (or virtue) are an end in themselves, external goods and goods of the body are merely a means to that end. Both reason and experience teach that virtue is not acquired by help of external goods, but external goods by help of virtue, and that happiness, whether consisting in pleasure or virtue or both, is more often found in those who are most highly cultivated in mind and character. There can be such a thing as too many external goods, but too much virtue never, and whereas external goods can be acquired by chance, virtue can only ever be acquired by serious thought. Happiness amounts to right actions and neither individual nor state can do right actions without virtue and wisdom. The happiness of the individual is the same as that of the state, since that which people wish for themselves they wish also for the state. The best state is that in which everyone can act best and live happily.

The question arises, which is to be preferred, the life of the philosopher or the life of the statesman? Clearly, the life of the freeman is better than the life of the despot, but not every sort of rule is despotic. If happiness is virtuous activity, then the active life is preferable to the inactive, both for the individual and for the city collectively. At the same time, virtuous activity is the product of serious thought, and the life of a statesman should go hand in hand with that of a philosopher.

A great city should not be confounded with a populous one, and a state should be judged not by the number, but by the power of its citizens, that is, by their ability to fulfil the work of the state. A very populous state is rarely well governed, whereas a state with a small population is not self-sufficient. If offices are to be distributed according to merit, then the citizens must know each other's characters, and the population of the state should not exceed that which can be taken in by the eye. As for population, so for territory: the territory should be all-producing and thereby self-sufficing, but it should not exceed that which can be taken in by the eye. It should be readily defensible and well situated in regard both to land and sea. Access to the sea leads to an undesirable influx of foreigners, but this is more than counterbalanced by increased trade and the services of a naval force. Any such trade should be carried out for the sake not of greed, but of self-sufficiency.

Although peoples from the North are full of spirit, they are lacking in intelligence and skill and therefore in political organisation. Peoples from the East are intelligent and inventive, but they are lacking in spirit and therefore they are in a state of subjection and slavery. The Hellenic race is intermediate in character, and is both high-spirited and intelligent. If the Hellenes could be formed into one state, they would rule the world. For a state to be self-sufficient it must provide a number of indispensible things, namely, food, crafts, arms, property, worship, and government. These six different functions should be assigned to different persons so as to enable the citizens to lead the life of leisure that is required for the cultivation of virtue. Thus, citizens should not engage in farming or in craftsmanship – which should be left to slaves and barbarians – but only in the four other functions. Citizens in their youth should carry arms, those in their middle age should govern, and those in their old age should worship the gods. Both private and public property should be held by citizens, as only producers of virtue should have a share in the state. As the state's inhabitants should be as healthy possible, the city should be situated so that it has an abundance of springs and fountains and so that it is exposed to easterly winds but sheltered from northerly ones. The houses in the city should be laid out in straight lines but in an irregularly regular pattern that combines beauty with security. Similarly, cities should have walls, but care should be taken to make them ornamental as well as defensive.

The state which is best governed is that with the greatest opportunity for happiness, which is the realisation and perfect exercise of virtue. There are three things which make men good and virtuous, namely, nature, habit, and reason, and these must be in harmony with one another. Equality consists in the same treatment of similar persons, and no government can stand which is not founded upon justice. All citizens should take turns in governing and being governed, and all should be educated to become good men, for the things that are best for individuals are best also for states. The soul of man is divided into two parts, one that is rational and commanding, and another that lacks reason but that is able to obey the rational and commanding part. The first, rational part of the soul can itself be divided into two parts, one that is practical and another that is speculative, and it is this speculative part that is the better and the end.

> *For men must be able to engage in business and go to war, but leisure and peace are better; they must do what is necessary and indeed what is useful, but what is honourable is better. On such principles children ... should be trained. ...Even the Hellenes ... do not appear to have framed their governments with a regard to the best end, or to have given them laws and education with a view to all the virtues, but in a vulgar spirit have fallen*

> *back on those which promised to be more useful and profitable. ...If it be disgraceful in men not to be able to use the goods of life, it is peculiarly disgraceful not to be able to use them in time of leisure – to show excellent qualities in action and war, and when they have peace and leisure to be no better than slaves.*

Although reason is the end of man, habit should be taught before reason, for the irrational is prior to the rational, and a young child is driven more by his appetites than by reason and understanding. Men and women should marry in the prime of life; women should marry at about 18 years old, men at about 37. Men should not beget children much after the prime of their intelligence, that is, about 50 years old. Young children should be fed milk, encouraged to move about, inured to the cold, and protected from anything that is bad, indecent, or vulgar. Education should take place in two periods, from the age of 7 to puberty, and thereon to the age of 21.

Book 8

The education of the citizens should match the character of the constitution, for the character of democracy creates democracy, and the character of oligarchy creates oligarchy; the better the character, the better the government. As the entire city has but one end, education should be the same for all, and should be public rather than private. Children should be taught those useful things that are really necessary, but not all useful things, and in particular not those that are vulgar. By 'vulgar' is meant those that tend to deform the body or that lead to paid employment. All paid employment absorbs and degrades the mind.

The four traditional branches of education are (1) reading and writing, (2) gymnastics, (3) music, (4) drawing. The Ancients included music not for the sake of utility but for that of intellectual enjoyment in leisure. Unlike music, reading and writing and drawing have utility, but they also have liberal applications. In particular, reading and writing can open up other forms of knowledge, and drawing can lead to an appreciation of the beauty of the human form. Leisure should not be confused with amusement and relaxation, which are the antidotes to effort and exertion. The busy man strives for an end that he has not yet attained, but happiness is the end. Thus, happiness is experienced not by busy men, but by those with leisure. That which is noble should come before that which is brutal. Courage is more a function of nobility than of ferocity, and to turn children into athletes risks injuring their forms and stunting their growth. For these reasons, children should practice nothing more strenuous than light gymnastics. Following the onset of puberty, three years should be spent in study, and only after this triennium may a youth engage in hard exercise. However, the youth should guard against labouring both mind and body at the same time, as they are inimical to each other.

Returning to the subject of music, it is not easy to determine its nature, nor why anyone should have knowledge of it. Perhaps music, like sleep or drinking, offers nothing more than amusement and relaxation. Perhaps it promotes virtue. Or perhaps it contributes to the enjoyment of leisure and to mental cultivation. Some say that no freeman should play or sing unless he is intoxicated or in jest; rather than learning music, why not simply enjoy the pleasure and instruction that come from hearing it from others? Our considered opinion is that children should learn music so that they might become performers and critics, but their musical education should not extend too far beyond an appreciation of rhythm and harmony, and not to instruments such as the flute or lyre which require great skill but contribute nothing to the mind.

> *In addition to this common pleasure, felt and shared in by all ... may [music] not have also some influence over the character and the soul? It must*

have such an influence if characters are affected
by it. And that they are so affected is proved in
many ways, and not least by the power which the
songs of Olympus exercise; for beyond question
they inspire enthusiasm, and enthusiasm is an
emotion of the ethical part of the soul. Besides,
when men hear imitations, even apart from the
rhythms and tunes themselves, their feelings
move in sympathy. Since then music is a pleasure,
and virtue consists in rejoicing and loving and
hating aright, there is clearly nothing which we
are so much concerned to acquire and to cultivate
as the power of forming right judgments, and of
taking delight in good dispositions and noble
actions. Rhythm and melody supply imitations
of anger and gentleness, and also of courage and
temperance, and of all the qualities contrary to
these, and of the other qualities of character, which
hardly fall short of the actual affections...

CHAPTER 3

Rhetoric

It is absurd to hold that a man ought to be ashamed of being unable to defend himself with his limbs but not of being unable to defend himself with speech and reason, when the use of reason is more distinctive of a human being than the use of his limbs.

Book 1

1. Rhetoric is the counterpart of dialectic: both are faculties for providing arguments, neither is concerned with a definite subject. The study of rhetoric is the study of modes of persuasion. People are most fully persuaded of a thing if they consider that thing to have been demonstrated, for which reason persuasion is tantamount to demonstration. The demonstration of the orator is a sort of syllogism called an enthymeme, and the study of syllogisms is the subject of dialectic. Rhetoric is useful because some audiences cannot be persuaded by knowledge alone. Nonetheless, men have a natural instinct for truth, and that which is true and that which is good tends to be easier to prove and easier to believe in. The rhetorician should be able to take up both sides of an argument, not so as to make people believe that which is

wrong, but with the aim of understanding all the arguments and confuting his opponents. Rhetoric may do great harm if used unjustly, but this is also true of all good things with the one exception of virtue. Of course, the artful use of rhetoric by the skilled rhetorician does not necessarily lead to persuasion, just as the artful use of medicine by the skilled physician does not necessarily lead to health. But the use of rational speech is more distinctive of man that the use of his limbs. Just as man is able to defend himself with his limbs, so he should be able to defend himself with his speech and with his reason.

2. Rhetoric may be defined as the ability, in any given case, to see the available means of persuasion. There are three technical means of persuasion that are (1) in the personal character of the speaker (*ethos*), (2) in the emotional state of the audience (*pathos*), (3) in the argument itself (*logos*). Their mastery requires the ability to understand human character and goodness, the ability to understand the emotions, and the ability to reason logically. A speaker is more persuasive if he appears to be credible, and his credibility should derive not from people's opinions of him but from the speech itself. A speaker is more persuasive is he succeeds in stirring the emotions, since people's judgements are not the same when they are pleased and friendly as when they are pained and hostile. And a speaker is more persuasive if he is able to construct sound arguments, which may produce persuasion either by induction or by deduction (syllogism). If the proof of a proposition is based on a number of similar cases, then this is induction in dialectic and example in rhetoric; if it is based on certain other propositions being true, this is syllogism in dialectic and enthymeme in rhetoric. Although speeches that rely on enthymeme are no more persuasive than those that rely on example, they do tend to excite the louder applause.

3. There are three divisions of rhetoric: political or deliberative, legal or forensic, and ceremonial or epideictic. Political oratory urges either to do something or not to do something, and is concerned with the future; legal oratory

either attacks somebody or defends somebody, and is concerned with the past; ceremonial oratory either praises somebody or censures somebody, and is concerned with the present. Political oratory aims above all at establishing the expediency or inexpediency of some course of action, legal oratory at the justice or injustice of some action, and ceremonial oratory at the honour or dishonour of some person. These then are the three ends of the three divisions of rhetoric (Table 3). The orator should not lose sight of them.

Table 3: The Three Divisions of Rhetoric

Division	Content	Time	End
Political (deliberative)	Exhortation/ Dehortation	Future	Expediency/ Inexpediency
Legal (forensic)	Accusation/ Defence	Past	Justice/ Injustice
Ceremonial (epideictic)	Praise/Censure	Present	Honour/ Dishonour

4. The political orator deals not with things which definitely will take place or which cannot possibly take place, but only with those that may or may not take place and, additionally, that are in our influence. The five most common topics of political oratory are ways and means (finance), war and peace, national defence, imports and exports, and legislation. The political orator needs to have detailed information about each of these topics.

5–7. In Chapter 5, Aristotle argues that men aim at an end which determines what they choose and what they avoid, and that this end is happiness. He then proceeds to describe the various constituents of happiness. In Chapter 6, he specifies that political oratory seeks not ends in themselves but means to ends. In other words, political oratory seeks utility. As utility is a good thing, he proceeds to describe the various constituents of the good. And as people often disagree about which of two things is the more useful and hence the better, he also discusses relative goodness, which is the subject of Chapter 7.

8. The most important qualification for political oratory is an understanding of all the forms of government and their respective customs, institutions, and interests. The forms of government are four: democracy, wherein offices of state are distributed by lot; oligarchy, wherein there includes a qualification of property; aristocracy, wherein there includes a qualification of education; monarchy, wherein offices of state are held by one man, who sits either as king or as tyrant. Men choose their means with reference to their ends, and the four forms of government each have a different end. The end of democracy is freedom; of oligarchy, wealth; of aristocracy, the maintenance of education and national institutions; of tyranny, the protection of the tyrant.

9. The ceremonial orator is concerned with virtue and vice, praising the one and censuring the other. The forms of virtue are justice, courage, temperance, magnificence, magnanimity (doing good to others on a large scale), liberality, gentleness, prudence, wisdom. The forms of vice are their opposites. Things that are productive of virtue are noble, as are the effects of virtue. Indeed, anything that is esteemed can be represented as being noble. There are a number of rhetorical devices for heightening the effects of praise, for example, emphasising that a man is the first or only one to have done something, or that he has done it better than anyone else.

10. The legal orator should have studied 'wrong-doing', which is defined as 'injury voluntarily inflicted contrary to law'. He should have ascertained the nature and number of incentives to wrong-doing, the states of mind of wrongdoers, and the kinds of persons who are wronged as well as their condition. In considering the motives and states of mind of wrong-doers, the seven possible causes of any action are enumerated: chance, nature, compulsion, habit, reasoning, anger, and appetite.

11. As all voluntary actions must either be or seem to be good or pleasant, it is important to ascertain the number and nature of things that are either useful or pleasant. The useful has already been examined in Chapter 6 in connexion with political oratory, so there remains only to examine the pleasant. Pleasure is a movement by which the soul is consciously brought into its normal or natural state of being, and pain is the opposite. Habits are pleasant because that which becomes habitual becomes quasi natural. In contrast, force is unnatural, and it follows that that which is compulsory is also unpleasant. Also pleasant is that which is desired, since desire is nothing more than the craving for pleasure. That which is pleasant may well be present and perceived, but it may also be past and remembered, or future and expected. The pleasant that is past and remembered may have been pleasant at the time, but this is not necessarily so. Wherefore the axiom, 'Sweet 'tis when rescued to remember pain...' Aristotle goes on to describe a number of pleasurable things, including anger, revenge, love, and learning.

12. Having considered the motives that make people do wrong, Aristotle discusses the states of mind in which they do it, and the kinds of people to whom they do it. First of all, the wrong-doer must suppose that his crime can be accomplished and that it can be accomplished by him. Moreover, he must suppose that he is able to escape discovery or punishment, or that punishment is less than the advantage of wrong-doing. He is more likely to think that he can escape punishment if he has one or more of eloquence, practical ability, legal expertise, many friends, much money. Also if he is on good terms with either his victims or his judges, if he has no enemies or a great many, if he hides his crime, if he has often escaped detection or punishment, and so on. The kinds of people whom he is most likely to wrong include those who possess that which he covets, those who are trustful, those who are too easy-going to prosecute or who have been severally wronged but have never prosecuted, and those who are hated or unpopular.

13. Just and unjust actions may be classified in relation to (1) the law, (2) the persons affected. Particular law is laid down by a community, whereas universal law is given by nature and is eternal. Certain actions, such as avoiding military service, affect the entire community, whereas others, such as adultery or assault, affect only certain of its members. The doer of an action must either intend or not intend it. If he intends it, he must act either from deliberate purpose or from passion. It is deliberate purpose that constitutes criminal guilt, and it should be possible to distinguish between criminal acts that are due to badness and those that are due to errors of judgement or to misfortunes.

> *Equity bids us be merciful to the weakness of human nature; to think less about the laws than about the man who framed them, and less about what he said than about what he meant; not to consider the actions of the accused so much as his intentions, nor this or that detail so much as the whole story; to ask not what a man is now but what he has always or usually been.*[1]

14. The worse of two bad acts is usually that which is prompted by the worse disposition, even if it is the slighter, and the converse is true of just acts. This is because the greater is potentially contained in the lesser. Sometimes, however, the worse act is simply that which results in the greatest harm. A man's crime is made worse if he is the only one to have committed it, if this is not the first time that he has committed it, if it is especially brutal or deliberate, if it stirs up more terror than pity, if it has required measures to prevent or punish similar crimes, if it has been committed in a place· where criminals are punished. The legal orator should demonstrate

1 Translated by W. Rhys Roberts.

that, in committing the crime, the man has broken not one but several solemn obligations.

15. Then there also the 'non-technical' means of persuasion that pertain especially to legal oratory. These are five in number: laws, witnesses, contracts, tortures, oaths. Aristotle discusses each one in turn. If the written law is unfavourable to the orator's case, then he must appeal to the universal law as Antigone did when she pleaded that in burying her brother she had broken Creon's law but not the unwritten law, which, in contrast to the written law, is changeless and eternal. Or he may argue that the law in question contradicts itself, or that it contradicts some other law, or that it is open to interpretation, or that it is antiquated. Witnesses may be either recent witnesses or, better still, ancient witnesses such as Solon, Homer, or a proverb. If the orator has no witnesses of fact, he can always call upon witnesses of character to prove either his worth or the worthlessness of his opponent.

Book 2

1. Having considered the nature of the arguments (*logos*) to be used in political, legal, and ceremonial oratory, Aristotle goes on to discuss the emotional state of the audience (*pathos*) and the personal character of the speaker (*ethos*), which are also important means of persuasion. The correct *pathos* is particularly important in legal oratory, and the correct *ethos* in political oratory. The three things that inspire confidence in the character of the orator are (1) good sense, (2) good moral character, and (3) goodwill, as the lack of any one of these may lead to false statements or bad advice. How to seem sensible and morally good can be deduced from the prior analysis of goodness. The analysis of goodwill and friendliness is yet to come, to be contained within the discussion of the emotions. The emotions are those feelings that are attended by pain or pleasure, and that so change people as to affect their judgements. For every emotion, the orator must consider three things: (1) the state of mind that accompanies it, (2) the

71

persons to whom it is directed, and (3) the grounds on which it is held.

2. Anger is an impulse, accompanied by pain, to a conspicuous revenge for a conspicuous slight that has been directed either at oneself or at one's friends. It is also attended by a certain pleasure which arises from the expectation of revenge. To slight someone is to entertain the opinion that he is obviously of no importance. There are three kinds of slight: contempt, spite, and insolence. The more a person is distressed – for example, in poverty or in love – the more he is prone to anger, and all the more if it is his distress itself that is slighted, and all the more still if he had been expecting a contrary result. A person's anger is all the stronger if he is insecure about the particular qualities and abilities that have been slighted, or if he has been slighted by someone who had previously treated him with courtesy and respect. Particularly offensive is for the person to have been slighted by someone who is clearly his inferior, or to have been slighted in the presence of five classes of people: his rivals, those who he admires, those by whom he wishes to be admired, those who he reverences, those who reverence him. A person is angry with his friends if they do not speak well of him or treat him well, or if they do not perceive his needs. And he is angry at all those who are indifferent to the pain that they give him, who ignore or rejoice at his misfortunes, who listen to stories about him or keep on looking at his weaknesses, and so on. The orator should speak so as to represent his adversaries as deserving of anger.

3. The opposite of anger is calmness, which can be defined as a quieting of anger. Since a person feels angry at those who slight him, it is plain that he feels calm at those who do nothing of the kind, or who do it involuntarily, or who intend the opposite of what they do, or who treat themselves in a similar fashion, or who admit their fault and are sorry, or who humble themselves before him and behave like his inferior. Even dogs do not bite sitting people. A person feels no anger

at those who are serious when he is serious, or who have done him more kindnesses than he has done them, or who reverence him, or who he fears and respects. He feels no or comparatively little anger at those who slight him out of anger. The frame of mind that makes people calm is plainly the opposite to that which makes them angry. Thus, people are calm when they are feeling prosperous or successful, satisfied, or otherwise free from pain. Anger is calmed by time, and by being spent on someone or other. People were angrier at Ergophilius than at Callisthenes, but they acquitted Ergophilius because they had already condemned Callisthenes to death. People also become calm if they have convicted the offender, or if he has already suffered enough, or if they feel that they deserved to be slighted. As anger has to do with individuals, no one gets angry at those who cannot become aware of their anger or at those who are dead. The poet who wrote, 'Say it was Odysseus, sacker of cities,' thereby implied that Odysseus would not have considered himself avenged unless the Cyclops perceived both by whom and for what he had been blinded.

4. Friendliness towards a person is to wish for him what one believes to be good things, and to be inclined to bring these things about. Friends are those who feel this way about each other. By having the same wishes and wishing for each other that which they wish for themselves, they show each other that they are friends. A person feels friendly to those who have treated him well or who wish to treat him well, to the friends of his friends, and to the enemies of his enemies, in short, to all those who share in the same or in similar notions of good and evil. In particular, he feels friendly to those who are virtuous, for example, those who are liberal, brave, or just, and to those with whom it is pleasant to live and spend one's days, for example, those who are good-tempered and who do not nurse grudges. A person does not feel friendly to those with whom he feels uncomfortable or of whom he feels frightened.

The opposite of friendship is enmity. Whereas anger arises from offences against the self, enmity arises even in their absence, and a person may hate another simply on the basis of character. Thus, whereas anger has to do only with individuals, hatred may also have to do with classes, for example, the class of thieves rather than one single thief. Anger aims at pain, hatred at harm; the angry person feels pain, the hater not at all. Time can quell anger, but it cannot quell hatred. From this exposition the orator can prove people to be friends or enemies, or refute their claims to friendship or enmity, or attribute their actions to either anger or hatred.

5. Fear is pain or disturbance due to a mental image of some future evil that is itself either painful or destructive. No one is frightened by an evil which is neither painful nor destructive, or by an evil which appears remote. Fear can be brought about by the indication of some painful or destructive future evil, such as the anger or enmity of people with the power to harm us, or, indeed, anyone with the power to harm us – for if they can, they often will. Generally speaking, anything that happens or threatens to happen to other people and that inspires pity also inspires fear. At the same time, there is no fear unless there is also at least the illusion of some small chance of escape.

The opposite of fear is confidence, namely, the expectation associated with a mental image of the presence of that which is protective combined with the absence or remoteness of that which is threatening. A person feels confident if he feels able to dispel or to prevent trouble, if he has not wronged or been wronged, if he has no rivals or only puny ones, if his rivals are his friends, if those who share his interests are numerous or strong or both. He also feels confident if he believes that he has often been successful, or that he has often escaped danger. Anger breeds confidence because an angry person feels that he has been wronged and therefore that the divine power is on his side.

6. Shame is a pain or disturbance in regard to bad things which seem likely to bring discredit either to us or to those whom we care for; shamelessness is disregard for or indifference to

the same. The bad things in question are those related to moral badness, for example, cowardice, injustice, flattery, effeminacy, or boastfulness; to lacking in honourable things shared by others like ourselves, especially if this is through own fault (in which case it is due to our moral badness); to having done to us acts that involve dishonour or reproach. Before strangers we are more ashamed of conventional faults, whereas before intimates we are more ashamed of genuine ones.

7. Kindness is helpfulness towards a person in need, not for one's own sake but for his. Kindness is great if it is towards a person in great need or in need of something important and hard to get, or if one is the only, first, or chief person to demonstrate it. To make a person appear unkind, the orator should argue that he was helpful for his own sake, that his act was accidental or compelled, or that he was merely returning a favour.

8. Pity is a feeling of pain caused by a painful or destructive evil that befalls one who does not deserve it, and that might well befall us or one of our friends, and, moreover, to befall us soon. Thus, it is not felt by those who no longer have anything to lose, or by those who feel that they are beyond misfortune. Pity is all the stronger if evil is repeated frequently or if it arises from a source from which good could have been expected. It may also be felt if no good ever befalls a person, or if he cannot enjoy it when it does, or if it does only once the worst has already happened. A person feels pity for those who are like him and for those whom he knows, but not for those who are very closely related to him and for whom he feels as he does for himself. Indeed, the pitiful should not be confounded with the terrible: Amasis wept at the sight of his friend begging, but not at that of his son being led to death. To feel pity, one must believe in the goodness of at least some people, which is why pity is most commonly felt by the young, and most sharply for those of noble character.

9. The opposite of pity is indignation, which may be defined as pain at unmerited good fortune. Indignation is not the same

as envy, which is pain at the good fortune of our equals. If good or bad fortune is merited, then the honest person should feel neither pity nor indignation but only satisfaction. Indignation is felt more keenly if a person's good fortune is recent rather than long established, if his good fortune seems inappropriate for him, or if by his good fortune he pretends to contend with his superior. It is also felt more keenly by those who think that they deserve the greatest possible goods and moreover have them, by those who are really good and honest, and by those who are ambitious – in short, by all those who think that they deserve something when others do not. Conversely, those who are servile, unambitious, or worthlessness are not prone to indignation.

10. Envy is pain at the good fortune of equals. It is felt if a person has, or thinks that he has, equals; if he is only a little short of having everything; if he has, or aims at, a reputation for some particular thing; if the having of the thing in question puts him slightly above other people or the not having it, slightly below. Those who are envied are those who are near in time, place, and status, 'for we do not compete with men … who live near the Pillars of Hercules'. Envy is particularly common in small-minded people to whom everything seems great, and it is felt most sharply when the success of an equal makes it clear that our failure is our own fault. If the orator instils envy into his hearers, these will no longer be able to feel pity.

11. Emulation is pain at the presence in others of good things that are absent in ourselves; this pain is not due to others having these good things, which is envy, but to us ourselves not having them. Unlike envy, emulation is a good thing because it makes us take steps towards securing good things. It is keenly felt by those who believe themselves to deserve certain good things that they do not yet have, and more keenly still by the young and those of an honourable or lofty disposition. It is felt most of all for anything that is especially honoured, such as moral goodness or things that

are useful and serviceable, for example, power or wealth rather than health. The opposite of emulation is not envy but contempt, and those who emulate or who are emulated are naturally disposed to be contemptuous of those who have bad things or who have good things through luck rather through just desert.

12. After having discussed the emotions Aristotle moves on to discuss the various types of human character, beginning with the young. The young have strong but changeable passions. They are quick tempered and lacking in self-control, and this makes them all the more likely to yield to their passions. They are eager for superiority and easily feel slighted. They love honour and victory more than money, and would rather do noble deeds than useful ones. As the greater part of their life lies before them, they live more in expectation than in memory; and as they are lacking in experience, they have exalted notions and tend to see the good rather than the bad. Although they are confident and courageous, they are still accepting of the rules of their society; and although they like spending their days with others, they have not yet learned to value their friends for their usefulness. They are quick to pity because they think that everyone is honest. If they wrong others, this is more to insult than to do real harm. As they are fond of fun, they are witty – wit being nothing other than well-bred insolence. They think they know everything and so they overdo everything. This is the source of all their mistakes.

13. In contrast to the young, the elderly live by memory rather than by hope. As they have a lot of experience, they are sure about nothing and under-do everything. They are small-minded because they have been humbled by life. As a result, they are driven too much by the useful and not enough by the noble. They are cynical and distrustful and neither love warmly nor hate bitterly. They are not shy but rather shameless, and feel only contempt for people's opinion of them. As that which is desired most strongly is that which is needed

most urgently, they love life, and all the more when their last day has arrived.

14. The body is in its prime from thirty to thirty-five; the mind at about forty-nine. The character of people in their prime is between that of the young and that of the elderly. Thus, people in their prime are neither overly confident nor overly timid, neither trustful nor mistrustful, and driven both by what is noble and by what is useful. 'To put it generally, all the valuable qualities that youth and age divide between them are united in the prime of life, while all their excesses or defects are replaced by moderation and fitness.'

15–17. Aristotle next considers those gifts of fortune by which human character is affected, namely, good birth, wealth, and power. The effect of good birth, that is, of ancestral distinction, is to make people more ambitious. However, to be well born is not to be noble, and most of the well born are wretches nonetheless. 'In the generations of men as in the fruits of the earth, there is a varying yield; now and then, where the stock is good, exceptional men are produced for a while, and then decadence sets in.' A clever stock will degenerate towards insanity, as did the descendants of Alcibiades, whereas a steady stock will degenerate towards torpor, as did the descendants of Pericles and of Socrates. The effect of wealth is to make people more arrogant and insolent. They come to imagine that there is nothing that their wealth cannot buy. Indeed, when Hiero's wife asked whether it was better to grow rich or to grow wise, Simonides replied that it was better to grow rich because wise men spend all their days at rich men's doors. In short, wealth turns a man into a prosperous fool, and all the more so if it has been recently acquired. The effect of power is to make people aspire to the great deeds that lie within their grasp. The respect that they receive and the responsibility that they owe make them more moderate, more serious, and more dignified – with dignity being a mild and becoming form of arrogance.

18–20. Aristotle discusses the arguments common to all oratory, namely, the topics of the possible and impossible, fact past, fact future, and size or degree, before moving on to the general principles of arguing by example and by enthymeme. The argument by example has the nature of induction, which is the foundation of reasoning. It has two varieties, one concerning past facts, and the other concerning the invention of facts by the orator. The latter again has two varieties, the illustrative parallel and the fable. Fables such as those of Aesop or those from Libya are comparatively easy to invent and are suitable for addresses to popular assemblies. However, in political oratory it is often more useful to quote past facts, as in most respects the future will resemble the past. If an orator can argue by enthymeme, then he should only use examples as subsequent supplemental evidence, in effect turning his examples into witnesses.

21. A maxim is a statement of a general kind about questions of practical conduct, whereas an enthymeme is a deduction dealing with such practical subjects. Thus, it is roughly true that the premises or conclusions of enthymemes are maxims. Maxims are only appropriate for elderly men with experience of the subject in hand; it is unbecoming for young men to utter maxims. The greatest advantage of the maxim is that it invests a speech with character. Another great advantage of the maxim is that people love to hear expressed in general terms that which they already believe in some particular connexion. For instance, a man who has bad children will happily agree with anyone who tells him, 'Nothing is more foolish than to be the parent of children.' Maxims that declare something to be universally true when it clearly is not can be used to stir up feelings of horror and indignation. For instance, an orator who is calling upon his men to risk an engagement in the absence of favourable omens might say, 'One omen of all is best, that we fight for our fatherland.' Some proverbs are also maxims, and their contradiction can heighten people's opinion of the character of the orator. For instance, the orator might say, 'We

ought not to follow the saying that bids us treat our friends as future enemies: much better to treat our enemies as future friends.'

22. An orator who uses the enthymeme must know at least some and preferably all of the facts of the subject in hand. There are two varieties of enthymeme, one that proves some affirmative or negative proposition, and another that disproves one. The difference between the two is the same as that between deduction and refutation in dialectic. The probative enthymeme makes an inference from that which is accepted, the refutative from that which is unaccepted.

23. One commonplace is the consideration of the opposite of the thing in question. If this opposite has the opposite quality, then the orator establishes the original proposition. For instance, 'Temperance is beneficial, for licentiousness is hurtful.' Another commonplace is the consideration of some modification of the key-word, and the arguing that that which can or cannot be said of the one also can or cannot be said of the other. For instance, "Just' does not always mean 'beneficial', or 'justly' would always mean 'beneficially', whereas it is *not* desirable to be justly put to death.' Another is based on correlative ideas. For instance, if a person gave just or noble treatment to another, the orator could argue that the other must have received noble or just treatment. Another is the *a fortiori*, according to which if the less likely thing is true, then the more likely thing is also true. For instance, the orator could argue that the man who strikes his father also strikes his neighbours. Conversely, the orator could argue that if the more likely thing is not true, then the less likely is also not true. This form of argument can even be used in a case of parity. For instance, 'If Hector did well to slay Patroclus, Paris did well to slay Achilles.' Another is to return an accusation to the accuser, so long as he is the more likely to commit the deed. For instance, 'Would *you* take a bribe to betray the fleet? No? Well, if you would not, why would I?' Another is secured by defining terms and then using the result to reason on the

point at issue. For instance, in refusing to go to the court of Archelaus, Socrates said, 'One is insulted by being unable to requite benefits, as well as by being unable to requite injuries.' Another is founded upon logical division, for instance, 'All men do wrong from one of three motives, A, B, and C: in my case A and B are out of the question, and even my accusers do not allege C.' Another is based upon induction, for instance, 'If one does not hand over his horses to the care of men who have mishandled other people's horses, then...' Another is founded upon some decision already pronounced, for instance, Isocrates argued that Paris must have been a good man because the goddesses chose him before all others. Another consists in taking separately the parts of a subject, for instance, 'What temple has he profaned? What gods recognised by the state has he not honoured?' Another is to be selective in enumerating the consequences of something, for instance, 'Education leads to unpopularity. It is therefore not well to be educated.' This can also be done for two opposites, for instance, 'Do not take up public speaking, for if you say that which is right, men will hate you; if you say that which is wrong, the gods will hate you.' 'On the contrary, if I say that which is right, the gods will love me; if I say that which is wrong, men will love me.' Another is rational correspondence, for instance, 'If you count tall boys men, you will next be voting short men boys.' Another is to argue that if two results are the same, then their antecedents are also the same, for instance, according to Xenophanes, to assert that the gods are born is an impious as to say that they die because both have the consequence that there was a time when the gods did not exist. Another is based on the fact that men are not always consistent in their choices, for instance, 'When we were exiles, we fought to return; now that we have returned, it would be strange to choose exile in order not to fight.' Another is to assert that some possible motive for an event or state of affairs is the real one, for instance, that Diomede picked out Odysseus not to honour him (Odysseus) but so that his companion would be a lesser man than himself.

81

Another is to consider the motives – that is, inducements and deterrents – for doing or not doing something, for instance, an action is all the more likely if it is possible, easy, and useful to its doer. Another is to argue that something that is supposed to happen but that seems incredible must be true because people believe in it, for instance, 'Just as fish need salt and olive-cakes need oil, so the laws need a law to set them right.' Another is to consider how the accused may have taken a better course of action, and to argue that no one voluntarily and knowingly chooses that which is bad. Another is to argue that the presence or absence of the cause entails the presence or absence of the effect. Another is to refute an opponent by noting any disagreements in his case. And so on. Of all the enthymemes, the most effective are those that are short and clear and those the conclusion of which, while not being entirely obvious, can yet be pleasurably anticipated by the hearers.

24. There are also enthymemes that look genuine but that are not. Spurious enthymemes may arise from the language that is used, for instance, from using the sort of language that is used for enthymemes or from using homonymy; from asserting of the whole that which is true only of the parts; from using indignant language; from using a sign that contains no deduction, as in, 'Dionysius is a thief, since he is a vicious man'; from using the accidental, as in, 'The mice came to the rescue because they gnawed through the bowstrings'; from arguing from consequence, as in, 'Paris must have had a lofty disposition since he despised society and lived by himself on Mount Ida'; from representing as causes things which are only coincidental; from leaving out any mention of time or circumstances; or from confusing that which is absolute from that which is not.

25. An argument may be refuted either by a counter-deduction or by an objection. The materials of deductions are reputable opinions; these often contradict each other, thereby providing also the materials for counter-deductions.

Such refutative enthymemes are no different from other enthymemes. An objection may be raised in one of four ways, attacking the statement, advancing another statement like it, advancing another statement contrary to it, quoting previous decisions. Enthymemes are based upon one of four things, probabilities, examples, signs, and evidences. Enthymemes based on probabilities can be refuted by raising some objection. However, the defendant must prove not only that the charge is not bound to be true, but also that it is not *likely* to be true. Enthymemes based on examples can be refuted in the same way as probabilities. If the defendant has a single negative instance, the argument is refuted; otherwise he must contend that the case in hand is dissimilar in some way or other. Enthymemes based on signs can be refuted simply on the basis that signs are non-deductive. Enthymemes based on evidence are impossible to refute in this way, and can only be refuted by showing that the alleged fact does not exist. If it is clear that it does, then refutation is impossible.

26. Having discussed the thought element of a speech, that is, the way to invent and to refute arguments, Aristotle proposes to discuss the language and arrangement of the speech. This is the subject of Book III.

Book 3

1. 'It is not enough to know what we ought to say; we must also say it as we ought...' Delivery has just as much to do with oratory as with drama, and is essentially a matter of expressing the various emotions by modulating volume, pitch, and rhythm.

2. To be good, style should be clear and should be plain. Speech should also be appropriate, that is, neither too base nor too elevated. An orator should use everyday speech but lend it an unfamiliar air. However, he should disguise his art and give the impression of speaking naturally. Strange words, compound words, and invented words should be used sparingly as they may make the speech seem too elevated.

In prose, apart from the proper terms for things, only metaphorical terms can be used with advantage. Metaphor is used in the course of normal conversation and, if fitting, brings clarity, charm, and distinction. A bad metaphor, for example, 'Calliope's screech' for 'poetry' or 'crimson-fingered morn' instead of 'rosy-fingered morn' may fail. A bad metaphor is one that is not fitting or that is not aesthetic in sound or meaning or imagery. If the orator wishes to praise, he should take a metaphor from something better in the same line; if to disparage, from something worse. For instance, for 'ask', the orator may take either 'pray' or 'beg'. Epithets such as 'father's avenger' or 'mother-slayer' for Orestes and diminutives such as 'cloaklet' for 'cloak' or 'plaguelet' for 'plague' can also make a good thing less good or a bad thing less bad.

3. Bad taste in language may take any of four forms. First is the inappropriate use of compound words, for instance, the face becoming 'flame-flushed' or the floor of the sea being 'sombre-hued'. Second is the use of strange words, for instance, 'spoliative' or 'witless'. Third is the use of inappropriate, long, or frequent epithets, for instance, 'monarchs of states' for 'laws' or 'the world-concourse of the Isthmian games' for 'the Isthmian games'. Fourth is the misuse of metaphor, that is, the use of metaphors that are ridiculous, overly theatrical, or obscure, for instance, 'events that are green and full of sap' or 'foul was the deed you sowed and evil the harvest you reaped'.

4. If it is said that 'the lion (Achilles) leapt', then this is a metaphor, but if it is said that 'Achilles leapt as a lion', then this is a simile. Although similes are of the nature of poetry, they can also be used in prose much as the metaphor. The simile and the metaphor are really the same thing, and the one can easily be turned into the other.

5. The foundation of good style is correctness of language, which has five elements: (1) the proper use and arrangement of connecting words or clauses, (2) the use of specific names rather than vague general ones, (3) the avoidance of ambiguity, (4) the observance of the gender of nouns, that is, male, female,

and inanimate, (5) the observance of number, that is, plurality, fewness, and unity. A composition should be easy to read and therefore easy to deliver; it should avoid (1) uncertainties as to punctuation, (2) zeugma,[2] (3) parenthesis.

6. The following suggestions should help to make language sound more impressive. (1) A thing can be described rather than named or, for concision, named rather than described. If its description is ugly, it should be named; if its name is ugly, it should be described. (2) A thing can be represented with metaphors and epithets, so long as poetical effects are avoided. (3) The plural can be used for the singular, as in, 'Unto havens Achaean'. (4) One article can be tied with each word or, for concision, two or more words can be bracketed under one article. (5) Plenty of connecting words can be used or, for concision, not many. Even then, connection should be preserved. (6) A thing can be described with attributes that it does not possess, for instance, 'a lyreless melody'.

7. Language is appropriate if it expresses emotion and character, and if it is suited to its subject. This aptness of language leads people to believe in the truth of a story.

8. The form of a prose composition should be neither metrical nor destitute of rhythm. The artificiality of the metrical form destroys trust and diverts attention. On the other hand, prose that is destitute of rhythm is both vague and unsatisfactory.

9. Prose can be either free-running, that is, of the kind that has no natural stopping-places, or compact and antithetical, of the kind that is in periods. The former is unsatisfying because its ending cannot be anticipated, whereas the latter is satisfying because it is easy to follow and to remember, and because people constantly feel as though they have grasped something. A period may be either simple or divided into several members, in which case it may be either simply divided or antithetical, for instance, 'These men used to sell

2   The joining of two or more parts of a sentence with a single common verb or noun.

you when they were at home, and now they have come to you here and bought you.' Such constructions have the effect of a logical argument. Parisosis is making the two members of a period equal in length. Paromoeosis is making the first or last words of the two members like each other.

10. A speech is lively if it enables us to get hold of fresh ideas quickly and easily. It is through metaphor and simile that ideas are most effectively conveyed. The simile is almost identical to the metaphor, but it is longer and less direct and so not as appealing. Of the four kinds of metaphor the most taking is the proportional kind, for instance, Leptines, speaking of the Lacedaemonians, said that he would not have the Athenians let Greece 'lose one of her two eyes'. Second, people are taken by arguments that the mind only just fails to keep up with, but not by arguments that are either too obvious or too difficult and lengthy. It is the antithetical form of argument that appeals most, for instance, 'judging that the peace common to all the rest was a war upon their own private interests'. Third, words ought to set the scene such that events are set before the eyes, in progress rather than in prospect.

11. To make people see events in progress rather than in prospect, the orator should use expressions that represent things as in a state of activity, for instance, 'Thereas up sprang the Hellenes to their feet,' or 'And the point of the spear in its fury drove full through the breastbone,' which contains both activity and metaphorical life. Liveliness is especially conveyed by metaphor and by surprising the hearer.

12. Each kind of rhetoric has its own appropriate style. The style of written prose is not that of spoken oratory, nor is the style of political speaking the same as that of legal speaking. The written style is more finished, but the spoken style better admits of dramatic delivery.

13. In terms of arrangement, a speech has two parts: stating a case, and then proving it. Statement and Argument are the only necessary parts of a speech, but Introduction and Epilogue can also be added.

14. The introduction is the beginning of a speech and corresponds to the prologue in poetry and to the prelude in flute music. In speeches of display, the orator should begin with that which best takes his fancy, and then strike up his theme and lead into it. In legal speeches, the orator should begin with a foretaste of the subject. If the subject is neither long nor intricate, then no introduction is required. Other kinds of introduction are remedial in purpose, aiming, for instance, at removing prejudice, arousing resentment, or gaining or distracting attention. People are ready to attend to anything that touches them or anything that is important, surprising, or agreeable. In some cases, it may be judicious to attract their attention at other points in the speech, for instance, by saying something like, 'Now I beg you to note this point – it concerns you quite as much as myself.' In political speeches the subject is usually familiar to the hearers and introductions are seldom required.

15. Various strategies for exciting or allaying prejudice are laid out. The orator may dispel objectionable suppositions or meet issues directly by denying or qualifying the alleged offence. For instance, Sophocles said that he was not trembling to make people think him an old man, but because he could not help it; he would rather not be eighty years old. Iphicrates replying to Nausicrates admitted that he had done the deed and that he had done Nausicrates harm, but not that he had done him wrong. The orator may draw attention to his calumniator's shortcomings, to others who have been accused by his calumniator and been found innocent, or to others who have been subject to the same accusation and been found innocent. He may also return calumny for calumny or denounce calumny, showing what an enormity it is, and in particular that it raises false issues. A method that is open to both calumniator and apologist is to select the motive that best suits his purposes. For instance, one might argue that Diomedes chose Odysseus as his companion because he supposed him to be the best of men, or because he

supposed him to be so worthless as to pose no threat at all. A method that is open to the calumniator is to praise some trifling merit at great length, and then attack some important failing concisely. This is the method of thoroughly skilful and unscrupulous prosecutors.

16. In ceremonial oratory, narration should be intermittent, as variety is pleasant but continuous narration is hard to keep in mind. In legal oratory, narration should be neither too concise nor too rapid, but rapid enough to achieve its purposes. As the orator goes along, he should slip in anything that does him credit or that does discredit to his adversary, and anything that the judges might enjoy. The defendant should make less of the narration, as he has to maintain that the thing has not happened, or did no harm, or was not unjust, or was not as bad as alleged. He should narrate events in the past tense, except where they excite pity and indignation by being narrated in the present tense. The narration should depict character, for example, by indicating moral purpose or by describing the manifestations of a certain type of character. Any detail that appears incredible should be explained, for instance, in the *Antigone*, Antigone says that she cared more for her brother than for husband or children because the latter could always be replaced whereas the former could not. The orator should make use of the emotions by relating their familiar manifestations, for instance, Aeschines described Cratylus as 'hissing with fury and shaking his fists'. 'These details carry conviction: the audience take the truth of what they know as so much evidence for the truth of what they do not.' In political oratory, there is very little opening for narration as nobody can narrate that which has not yet happened.

17. The duty of arguments is to attempt demonstrative proofs, which should bear directly upon the question in dispute. In legal oratory, the question in dispute may fall under one of four heads: the act was not committed, or if it was, it did no harm, it did less harm than alleged, or it was justified. In political oratory, it may be argued that a proposal

is impracticable, or unjust, or will do no good, or is not as important as its proposer thinks. Falsehoods about irrelevant matters should be highlighted, as they will look like proof that other statements are also false. In ceremonial oratory, the facts are usually well known or taken on trust, and it is argued that they are either useful or virtuous. Argument by enthymeme is highly suitable for legal oratory, and argument by example for political oratory. Refutative enthymemes are more popular than demonstrative ones because their logical cogency is more striking. A continuous succession of enthymemes should be avoided, or they will spoil one another's effect. Enthymemes should not be made on every point, nor should they be used to rouse feeling or to depict character. Both in legal and in political oratory, the first speaker should put his own arguments forward first and then tear apart his opponent's likely arguments – unless his opponent is likely to have a great variety of arguments, in which case he should begin with these. The second speaker should begin by attacking the first speaker's points. In buttressing his character, the orator may excite dislike, appear tedious, or expose himself to the risk of contradiction; in demolishing the character of his opponent, he may seem abusive or ill-bred. He should therefore put any such remarks in the mouth of some third person.

18. The best moment to use interrogation is when the opponent has so answered one question that the putting of just one more lands him in absurdity. Another good moment is when one of the opponent's premises is obviously true, and he must say 'yes' if he is asked whether another is true. For instance, when Meletus denied that Socrates believed in the existence of gods but admitted that he talked about a supernatural power, Socrates asked him whether supernatural beings were not either children of the gods or in some way divine. 'Yes,' said Meletus. 'Then,' replied Socrates, 'is there anyone who believes in the existence of children of the gods and yet not in the existence of the gods themselves?' A third good moment is when the opponent is contradicting his own

words or that which everyone believes. A fourth is when it is impossible for him to give anything but an evasive answer. In other cases interrogation should not be attempted. As to jests, jesting can be used to kill the opponent's earnestness, and earnestness to kill his jesting. Irony better befits a gentleman than buffoonery: the ironical man jokes to amuse himself, the buffoon to amuse other people.

19. The epilogue should achieve four things, to make the hearers well-disposed towards the orator and ill-disposed towards his opponent, to magnify or minimise the leading facts, to excite the required state of emotion in the hearers, and to summarise the arguments and thereby refresh their memories. For the conclusion, the disconnected style of language is appropriate and will mark the difference between the oration and peroration. 'I have done. You have heard me. The facts are before you. I ask for your judgement.'

CHAPTER 4

Poetics

*Poetry demands a man with a special gift for it, or
else one with a touch of madness in him.*

1–3. The *Poetics* treats of poetry in itself and of its various
kinds. Epic poetry, dithyrambic poetry, tragedy, comedy, and
the music of the flute and of the lyre in most of their forms are
all modes of imitation. However, they differ from one another
in respect to (1) the medium, (2) the objects, (3) the manner
or mode of imitation. The medium involves one or more of
language, rhythm, and harmony. Thus, the music of the flute
and of the lyre imitate by harmony and by rhythm, whereas
dancing imitates by rhythm alone. There is another art,
hitherto without a name, which imitates by language alone and
which includes the mimes of Sophron and Xenarchus and the
Socratic dialogues on the one hand, and the poetic imitations
in iambic, elegiac, or any similar meter on the other. Poetry is
not defined by verse form but by imitation or mimesis. Thus,
not everything that is written in verse is poetry, and poetry
may be written either in verse or in prose. In all kinds of poetry,
language, rhythm, and harmony are all used; in some cases,
such as lyric poetry, they are used together, whereas in others,
such as tragedy or comedy, they are used at different times.

The objects of imitation are men, whether of the higher or the lower type, and men should be represented as better than, worse than, or the same as in real life. Such diversities are found in all forms of poetry, even in dancing, flute-playing, and lyre-playing. In epic poetry and tragedy men are represented as better than in real life, in parody and comedy as worse. In terms of the manner of imitation, the poet may either employ third or first person narration, or present all of his characters as living and moving before us (drama).

4. Man is the most imitative of all the animals, and learns and derives pleasure from imitation. Even objects of pain such as dead bodies or ignoble animals become a delight if they are skilfully imitated. To learn and to reason is pleasurable not only to philosophers but to all men, even though their capacity for learning is less than that of philosophers. Another human instinct is that for rhythm and harmony, which finds its highest expression in poetry. Poets with a serious character imitate good and noble actions in hymns and epic poetry, the more trivial sort imitate the actions of baser and meaner persons in lampoons and satires. It is to these opposing tendencies that tragedy and comedy trace their origins.

5. Comedy, then, is an imitation of inferior characters. These characters are not bad in the full sense of the term, but merely ridiculous, that is, ugly or distorted and therefore neither painful nor destructive. Like tragedy, epic poetry is an imitation of superior characters, but, unlike tragedy, it employs only one kind of meter, it is in narrative form, and its action is not confined to a single day. Furthermore, whereas all the elements of epic poetry are found in tragedy, not all the elements of tragedy are found in epic poetry.

6. Tragedy is an imitation that is serious, complete, and of a certain magnitude; in language embellished by rhythm and harmony; in the form of action rather than narrative; arousing emotions of pity and fear and leading to the purification or purgation (*katharsis*) of these emotions. Tragedy requires not only song and diction but also a stage and some actors. An

actor is distinguished by character and by thought, since it is character and thought that give rise to actions, and it is on actions that success or failure depends. Thus, every tragedy has six parts which together determine its quality, namely, actions or plot (*mythos*), character, thought, diction, song, and spectacle. Of these six, plot is the most important of all. 'For tragedy is an imitation, not of men, but of an action of life, and life consists in action, and its end is a mode of action, not a quality.' Although it is a man's character that determines his qualities, it is by his actions that he is made happy or unhappy. Without plot there is no tragedy, but plenty of tragedies fail in the rendering of character. For both these reasons, character can only be second to plot. Third in order is thought, fourth is diction whether in verse or in prose, fifth is song, and sixth is spectacle.

7–9. A whole is that which has a beginning, a middle, and an end. Plot must not only be composed of these parts, but these parts need to be of a certain magnitude, for beauty depends on both order and magnitude. Magnitude should be such as can easily be taken in by the eye, or, in the case of a tragedy, by the memory. The action should be long enough for the main character to go from fortune to misfortune or *vice versa*: the longer the better, but not so long as to lose the audience.

Unity of plot does not consist in unity of the main character. Thus, in composing the Odyssey, Homer did not include all the adventures of Odysseus, but only those that form part of a single action (as broadly conceived). A thing whose presence or absence makes no apparent difference is not an organic part of the whole and therefore should not be included.

The poet should not relate what has happened but what may happen, that is, what is possible according to the law of probability or necessity. The poet differs from the historian not in that the one writes in verse whereas the other writes in prose, but in that the one relates what may happen whereas the other relates what has happened.

> *Poetry, therefore, is a more philosophical and a higher thing than history: for poetry tends to express the universal, history the particular ... It clearly follows that the poet or 'maker' should be the maker of plots rather than of verse; since he is a poet because he imitates, and what he imitates are actions. And even if he chances to take a historical subject, he is none the less a poet; for there is no reason why some events that have actually happened should not conform to the law of the probable and possible, and in virtue of that quality in them he is their poet or maker.*[1]

Actions should succeed one another with probability or necessity so as to provide insight into general principles regarding the conduct of human life. A tragedy is most effective at arousing feelings of fear and pity if actions come as a surprise, and yet succeed one another with probability or necessity. Even a coincidence can be rendered more striking if it is given an air of design, as in the case of the statue of Mitys at Argos which fell upon his murderer and killed him.

10–11. In a simple plot the change of fortune takes place without reversal of fortune (*peripeteia*) and without discovery or recognition (*anagnorisis*), whereas in a complex plot the change of fortune takes place with one or both of these elements. Reversal of the situation is a change from one situation to its opposite. For instance, in *Oedipus*, the messenger comes to free Oedipus from his alarms about his mother, but, by revealing who he is, he produces the opposite effect. Recognition is a change from ignorance to knowledge, bringing either hatred and misery or love and happiness. The best kind of recognition coincides with a reversal of the situation, as in *Oedipus*. Together they produce either pity or

1   Translated by SH Butcher.

fear, which is the aim of tragedy. In addition to reversal of the situation and recognition, a third part of the plot is the scene of suffering, which involves a destructive or painful action such as murder or mutilation.

12. The separate parts that are common to all plays of tragedy are prologue, episode, exode, and choric song (parode and stasimon). Some plays also have songs of actors from the stage and a *commos*, that is, a lamentation sung by both actors and chorus. The ordering of these parts is prologue, parode, episode, stasimon, exode. The parode is the first unbroken utterance of the chorus, the stasimon is a choral song without either anapests or trochaic tetrameters.

13. The plot of a perfect tragedy should be complex rather than simple, and it should imitate actions that excite pity and fear. The change of fortune should not involve a virtuous man passing from prosperity to adversity, for that does not inspire either pity or fear but merely shock. Nor should it involve a bad man passing from adversity to prosperity, for that does not contain any tragic element. Nor again should it involve the downfall of the utter villain; although this satisfies the moral sense, it does not inspire either pity or fear, for pity is inspired by unmerited misfortune, fear by the misfortune of a man who is like us. Instead, the change of fortune should involve a man who is neither bad nor eminently virtuous, but whose misfortune is brought about by some great error or frailty (*hamartia*). Furthermore, he must be illustrious like Oedipus, Thyestes, and others of that ilk.

The plot, although complex, should focus around a single issue. The change of fortune should not be from adversity to prosperity but from prosperity to adversity, and result not from vice but from some great error or frailty in a hero who is never worse, and often significantly better, than the average person. In days of yore tragedies were inspired by legends, but today the best are founded on the fortunes of a few houses, those of Alcmaeon, Oedipus, Orestes, Meleager, Thyestes, Telephus, and others who have done or suffered something terrible.

14. Fear and pity may be inspired by spectacle or, better still, by the plot itself, without any extraneous aids. Actions that particularly inspire fear and pity are those that occur between people who are near or dear to one another, rather than those that occur between people who are indifferent to one another or who are enemies. The action may be done consciously or out of ignorance. Alternatively, the protagonist may be about to act consciously but then does not act, or he may be about to act out of ignorance but then discovers the truth and does not act. Of the four, the worst is that in which he is about to act consciously and then does not act. Better if he does act, better still if he acts out of ignorance, and best if he is about to act out of ignorance but then discovers the truth and does not act.

15. The character of the tragic hero should be good, and this goodness should be revealed in a good moral purpose. 'Even a woman may be good, and also a slave; though the woman may be said to be an inferior being, and the slave quite worthless.' The good qualities of the hero should be appropriate to the character, for example, manly valour would be inappropriate in a woman. In addition to goodness and to propriety, the character should be true to life and he should be consistent; even if he is inconsistent, he should at least be consistently inconsistent. The actions of the tragic hero should be in keeping with his character such that the plot's denouement (*lusis*) arises from the plot itself and not from improbable events or divine intervention (*deus ex machina*). For the hero to be both true to life and good, it may be necessary to 'make a likeness which is true to life and yet more beautiful', as Homer does of Achilles in the *Iliad*.

16. There are six kinds of discovery or recognition (*anagnorisis*). The most common but least artistic is recognition by signs such as necklaces and bodily marks. Next is recognition so contrived that it breaks the unity of the plot. Third is recognition that depends on memory, such as when a disguised character breaks into tears upon seeing a picture or hearing a tune. Fourth is recognition that depends on a

false inference on the part of a disguised character. Fifth and second best is recognition by deductive reasoning such that the discovery is the necessary conclusion of a thought process. Sixth and best of all is recognition that arises from the actions themselves, as in the *Oedipus* of Sophocles.

17–18. In constructing the plot, the poet should picture the action in his mind so as to detect any possible inconsistencies. He should go so far as to enact the action so as to put himself into the shoes of his characters and to feel their emotions as they might. To do this, he requires either a happy gift of nature or a strain of madness. The poet should sketch a general outline of the plot before filling in its episodes. For instance, the general outline of the *Odyssey* can be rendered in just three sentences; all the rest is episode. Every tragedy consists of complication (*desis*) and of unravelling or denouement (*lusis*). The watershed between *desis* and *lusis* is *peripeteia* or reversal of fortune. There are four kinds of tragedy, namely, the complex, which depends entirely on *peripeteia* and *anagnorisis*, the pathetic in which the motive is emotional, the ethical in which the motive is moral, and the simple. As a tragedy could never successfully tell the entire story of the *Iliad*, the poet should focus on a single plot only and not on multiple plots as in epic poetry. He should regard the chorus as one of the actors, ensuring that it forms an integral part of the whole.

19–22. Thought is more thoroughly discussed in the *Rhetoric*. Suffice to say that under thought is included every effect which is produced by speech: proof and refutation, the excitation of the feelings, the suggestion of importance or its opposite. Unlike dramatic speeches, dramatic incidents should speak for themselves when evoking feelings.

The parts of diction include letter, syllable, conjunction, noun, verb, inflection or case, sentence or phrase. Aristotle goes on to define and to detail each of these parts.

Metaphor is the application of a name by transference either (1) from genus to species, (2) from species to genus, (3) from species to species, or (4) by analogy.

The perfection of style is to be clear without being mean. Language can be elevated from the meanness of ordinary words with strange words, compounded words, and metaphor. However, the use of such devices should be judicious, or else the composition may come to resemble jargon or a riddle, and to be not only unintelligible but grotesque and ludicrous. The command of metaphor is the greatest thing by far because it cannot be taught and implies an eye for resemblances, which is the mark of genius.

23–24. Epic poetry is narrative in form and employs a single meter. Like tragedy, it ought to be constructed on dramatic principles. It should comprise a single action that is an organic whole, with a beginning, a middle, and an end. A paradigm of the form is the *Iliad*, in which Homer focuses on a single portion of the Trojan War, and admits as episodes many events from the general story of the war.

Epic poetry should have as many kinds as tragedy, and may be simple or complex, pathetic or emotional. With the exception of song and spectacle, epic poetry requires the same six parts as tragedy, as well as *peripeteia* and *anagnorisis*. However, epic poetry is constructed on a larger scale than tragedy, and is narrated in elevated heroic meter rather than spoken in everyday iambic meter. Like Homer, who is in all respects admirable, the poet should speak as little as possible in his own person. Exaggerated or fantastic events stretch credulity to breaking point if performed on a theatrical stage, but not so if narrated in an epic poem. Even so, the irrational should be avoided or, at the very least, be made to appear credible.

25. Poetry may be criticised for lacking verisimilitude. However, exaggerated or fantastic events may be justified if their effect is to render the poem more striking. In other cases, the poet may be aiming to describe things not as they are, but as they ought to be, or as people say that they are. With regards to the requirements of art, a probable impossibility is to be preferred to an improbable possibility. Poetry may also

be criticised for contradictions arising from the language used. On closer inspection, however, these contradictions may not be real but only apparent, the product of metaphorical usage or some other poetic device. Criticism may also be levelled at an irrational plot or at a depraved character. Unless there is some inner necessity for introducing them, such criticism is entirely justified.

26. Unlike tragedy, epic poetry has no need to pander to its audience with ill-judged antics and histrionics. However, these faults pertain not to the poet but to the actors, and good tragedy can produce its effect even if it is not staged. Tragedy is superior to epic poetry because it is more vivid and more concentrated in its effect, more vivid because it has all the elements of epic poetry and also music and spectacle, and more concentrated because it has both greater unity and shorter length.

CHAPTER 5

Categories

Expressions which are in no way composite signify substance, quantity, quality, relation, place, time, position, state, action, or affection.

1. Things are named 'equivocally' if they share a name, and the definition of the name that they share differs for each. For instance, a real man and a figure in a picture both share the name 'animal', but the definition of 'animal' differs for each. On the other hand, things are named 'univocally' if they share a name, and the definition of the name that they share is the same for both. For instance, a man and an ox both share the name 'animal', and the definition of 'animal' is the same for both. Things are named 'derivatively' if they derive their name from another name, but differ from it in termination (i.e. if their names are paronyms). For instance, the grammarian derives his name from 'grammar', the courageous man from 'courage'.

2. Forms of speech are either simple, such as 'man' or 'runs', or composite, such as 'the man runs'.

Some things are predicable of (or 'said of') a subject, and never present in a subject, for instance, 'man' is predicable of the individual man.

By being 'present in a subject' I do not mean
present as parts are present in a whole, but being
incapable of existence apart from the said subject.[1]

Some things are present in a subject, and never predicable of a subject, for instance, a piece of grammatical knowledge is present in the mind, but is not predicable of any subject. Some things are predicable of a subject and present in a subject, for instance, knowledge is present in the mind and is predicable of grammar. Lastly, some things are not present in a subject and not predicable of a subject, for instance, the individual man or the individual horse.

3. Anything that is predicated of a predicate is also predicable of the subject, for instance, if 'man' is predicated of an individual man, and 'animal' is predicated of 'man', then 'animal' is also predicable of an individual man.

The differentiae of genera that are different and co-ordinate are themselves different in kind. For instance, differentiae of the genus 'animal' such as 'with feet', 'two-footed', 'winged', 'aquatic' are not the same as those of the genus 'knowledge'. On the other hand, there is nothing to prevent a genus and its subordinate from having the same differentiae.

4. Things that are said (*ta legomena*) can be divided into ten distinct kinds, (1) substance, (2) quantity, (3) quality, (4) relation, (5) place, (6) time, (7) position, (8) state, (9) action, and (10) affection. These are the ten categories or *praedicamenta*.

Simple forms of speech such as 'man', 'three cubits long', and 'white' do not by themselves constitute an affirmation, and therefore cannot be either true or false. For simple forms of speech to constitute an affirmation, they must be combined into statements.

5. A primary substance is that which is neither predicable of a subject nor present in a subject, for instance, the individual man or horse. A secondary substance is the species within

1   Translated by EM Edghill.

which a primary substance is included, for instance, 'man', and also the genera within which the species is included, for instance, 'animal'. A secondary substance such as 'man' can be predicated of a subject, and anything that can be predicated of 'man', for instance, 'animal', can also be predicated of that subject.

Those things that are present in a subject, for instance, 'white', are generally not predicable of the subject. In some cases the name 'white' is predicable of the subject; however, the definition of the colour white is never predicable of the subject.

Everything that is not a primary substance is either predicable of a primary substance or present in a primary substance. For instance, 'animal' is predicated of 'man' and therefore of the individual man; if there were no individual man of whom it could be predicated, it could not be predicated of 'man' at all. 'Colour' is present in body and therefore in individual bodies; if there were no individual body in which it could be present, it could not be present at all. If primary substances did not exist, it would be impossible for anything else to exist.

The most distinctive mark of substance is that, while remaining numerically one and the same, it is capable of admitting contrary qualities. Any such modification takes place not through statement or opinion, but through a change in the substance itself.

6. Quantity is either discrete, for instance, number and speech, or continuous, for instance, lines, surfaces, solids, time, and place. By definition, a continuous quantity has a common boundary at which its parts join.

Some quantities, for instance, lines, planes, solids, and space, are such that their parts have a relative position to one another; others, for instance, number, speech, and time, are not such.

Only the things above are intrinsically quantitative; things such as a lengthy action or process are quantitative only in a secondary sense.

Quantities have no contraries, for instance, 'two cubits long' has no contrary. It might be argued that 'large' and 'small' or 'much' and 'little' are contraries, but they have reference to an external standard and are therefore, properly speaking, relations rather than quantities.

The most distinctive mark of quantity is that equality and inequality can be predicated of it. For instance, a number can be said to be equal to another. By contrast, that which is not quantity cannot be spoken of in terms of equality and inequality. For instance, the quality of whiteness is compared to another quality not in terms of equality and inequality but of similarity.

7. A thing is relative if it is explained by reference to something else, for instance, the terms 'superior' and 'double' are relative, as a thing is superior to something else, or double of something else. Other relatives include habit, disposition, perception, knowledge, and attitude. Thus, habit is a habit of something, knowledge is knowledge of something, and so on.

Some relatives have contraries, for instance, knowledge and ignorance, but others do not, for instance, 'double'.

All relatives have a correlative, the correlative of 'slave' is 'master', and that of 'master' is 'slave'. If a mistake has been made, there is no longer this reciprocity of correlation. For instance, there is no reciprocity of correlation between 'wing' and 'bird' (as a bird is not a bird by reason of its wings), but only between 'wing' and 'winged creature'. If there is no word to express a correlation, it might be necessary to invent one, for instance, 'ruddered' for the correlation of 'rudder', 'headed' for the correlation of 'head'.

Most correlatives come into existence simultaneously, as in the case of the slave and the master, the double and the half. Correlatives that come into existence simultaneously cancel each other, for there cannot be a slave without a master, nor a master without a slave. Some correlatives do not come into existence simultaneously, for instance, knowledge comes into existence not at the same time as, but only after, the object of knowledge. Correlatives that do not come into existence simultaneously do not cancel each other, for, whereas there cannot be knowledge without the object of knowledge, there can well be the object of knowledge without knowledge.

No substance is relative, for the individual man or ox is not defined with reference to something external. Thus, whereas a relative can be apprehended by that to which it is relative, a substance cannot.

8. Quality can denote a number of things. One thing that it can denote is 'disposition' and its more permanent counterpart, 'habit'. Heat, cold, disease, health, and so on are dispositions, while the various kinds of knowledge and of virtue are habits. Another includes all those terms that refer to inborn capacity and incapacity such as hard and soft or that by which an athlete is a good or bad athlete. A third includes all those terms that refer to affective qualities and affections such as sweetness and sourness or whiteness and blackness. A fourth concerns shape, for instance, straight or curved, triangular or quadrangular.

The most distinctive mark of quality is that likeness and unlikeness can be predicated of it. If one thing is like or unlike another, then this is by virtue of a quality.

9. Action is to affection as the active voice is to the passive voice. Examples of actions are 'to lance' and 'to cauterise', examples of affections are 'to be lanced' and 'to be cauterised'.

Position is a condition of rest that results from an action, for instance, 'lying', 'sitting', 'standing'. It can also be understood as the relative positions of the parts of a thing. State is a condition of rest that results from an affection, for instance, 'shod', 'armed'.

Time and place are easily intelligible.

10–11. Having dealt with the proposed categories, it remains to explain the various senses of 'opposite'. Things might be opposed (1) as correlatives to one another, e.g. 'double' and 'half', (2) as contraries to one another, e.g. 'good' and 'bad', (3) as privatives to positives, e.g. 'blindness' and 'sight', (4) as affirmatives to negatives, e.g. 'he sits' and 'he does not sit'.

12. One thing might be prior to another in that (1) it is older or more ancient, (2) it comes first in an irreversible sequence, e.g. 'one' is prior to 'two', (3) it comes first in an order, e.g. in reading and writing the letters of the alphabet are prior to the syllables, in geometry the elements are prior to the propositions, (4) it is better and more honourable, (5) it is its cause, e.g. the fact of being a man is prior to the truth of the proposition that he is.

13. 'Simultaneous' is primarily applied to things that are generated simultaneously, for instance, 'double' and 'half'. Such things are simultaneous in point of time and in point of nature, as the being of each implies (although is not the cause of) the being of the other. Also simultaneous are those species that are distinguished from one another and opposed to one another within the same genus, for instance, the 'winged', the 'terrestrial', and the 'water' species.

14. There are six distinct sorts of movement: generation, destruction, increase, diminution, alteration, and change of place. Generally speaking, the contrary of movement is rest, but the different sorts of movement also have their own contraries, generation and destruction, increase and diminution, alteration and 'rest in its quality' or 'change in the direction of the contrary', change of place and 'rest in a place' or 'change in the reverse direction'.

15. 'To have' is used with respect to (1) habit or disposition or any other quality, e.g. to 'have' a piece of knowledge or a virtue, (2) quantity, e.g. to 'have' a certain height, (3) apparel e.g. to 'have' a coat or tunic, (4) something that is on a part of ourselves, e.g. to 'have' a ring on the hand, (5) something that is a part of ourselves, e.g. to 'have' a hand or a foot, (6) content, e.g. for a jar to 'have' wine, (7) acquisitions, e.g. to 'have' a house or field.

CHAPTER 6

On Interpretation

*A sea-fight must either take place tomorrow or not,
but it is not necessary that it should take place
tomorrow, neither is it necessary that it should not
take place, yet it is necessary that it either should
or should not take place tomorrow.*

1. Spoken words are the symbols of mental experience, and written words are the symbols of spoken words. These symbols may differ from one language to another, but the mental experiences that they symbolise are the same for all. Isolated nouns and verbs cannot be either true or false, for truth and falsity imply combination and separation.

2. A noun signifies a subject by convention, and without reference to time. The expression 'not-man' is not a noun nor is it a sentence or a denial. Let it be called an indefinite noun. The expressions 'of Philo', 'to Philo', and so on are not nouns, but cases of a noun. Coupling 'to be' with a noun yields a proposition that is either true or false; however, coupling 'to be' with a case of a noun, as in, 'of Philo is', does not.

3. A verb is a sign of something said of something else, and also carries with it the notion of time. For instance, 'health' is a noun, but 'is healthy' is a verb that indicates both health and its present existence. The expressions 'is not healthy', 'is

not ill', and so on, are not verbs, but indefinite verbs, since they apply equally to things that exist and to those that do not. Similarly, 'he was healthy' and 'he will be healthy' are not verbs, but tenses of a verb that indicate times outside the present. Verbs are substantive, but do not indicate anything unless something is added.

4. The parts of a sentence have an independent meaning as an utterance, but not as the expression of any positive judgement. Only when other words are added can the whole form an affirmation or denial. Although every sentence has meaning, not every sentence is a proposition. For instance, a prayer is a sentence, but it is not a proposition as it cannot be either true or false. Sentences that are not propositions and that cannot be either true or false belong not to the present study but to that of rhetoric or of poetry.

5. Every proposition must contain a verb or a tensed verb. A simple proposition asserts or denies something of something, and the conjunction of its parts gives a unity. A composite proposition is compounded of simple propositions.

6. An affirmation is a positive assertion of something about something, a denial a negative assertion. It is plain that every affirmation has an opposite denial and *vice versa*. Let such a pair of propositions be called a pair of contradictories. A pair of propositions are contradictories if they have the same subject and predicate, and if the identity of the subject and of the predicate are not equivocal.

7. Universal terms are those, such as 'man', that can be predicated of many subjects. By contrast, particular terms, such as 'Socrates', can only be predicated of one subject alone.

A positive and negative proposition of universal character, such as 'every man is white' and 'no man is white', are called *contrary*. A positive proposition of universal character and its non-universal denial, such as 'every man is white' and 'not every man is white', are called *contradictory*. Of contradictories, one must be true, the other false. Contraries also cannot both be true, although they can both be false, in which case their contradictories are both true. For instance, both 'every man is white' and 'no man is white' are false, but their contradictories, 'some men are not white' and 'some men are white' are both true. A single affirmation has a single negation.

8. An affirmation or denial is single if it indicates one fact about one subject, regardless of whether the subject or the proposition has a universal character e.g. 'every man is white'. If the word 'white' has two distinct meanings, then the affirmation is not a single one. For instance, if 'garment' signified both 'man' and 'horse', the proposition 'garment is white' would be equivalent to two simple propositions, namely, 'man is white' and 'horse is white'.

9. Of contradictory propositions about present and past, one must be true and the other false. However, if the subject is individual and the predicate is future, then this is not the case.

A sea-battle must either take place tomorrow or not, but it is not necessary that it should take place tomorrow, neither is it necessary that it should not take place. In such an instance one of the two propositions must be true and the other false, but which is true and which is false cannot as yet be determined and must be left undecided. In short, some future events are not necessary but contingent; unless this is so, nothing is uncertain or fortuitous, and it is futile to take trouble.

10. Every affirmation consists of a subject that is a noun, either definite or indefinite, and of a verb, also either definite or indefinite. The verb not only contributes its specific meaning but also the notion of time. The verb 'is' can be used either as a predicate signifying existence, as in 'a man is', or as a third element, as in 'man is just'. In the first case, only the subject can be made indefinite, and so only two affirmations can be formed, 'man is' and 'not-man is', as well as two corresponding negations, 'man is not' and 'not-man is not'. In the second case, both the subject and the predicate can be made indefinite, and so four affirmations can be formed, 'man is just', 'not-man is just', 'man is not-just', and 'not-man is not-

just', as well as four corresponding negations. If the verb is not 'is' but, say, 'walks' or 'enjoys health', then it is simply as if 'is' had been joined on.

11. The unity of a proposition is lost if the proposition predicates one thing of many subjects, or many things of the same subject – unless the many are really indicating one thing. Some predicates can combine to form a composite predicate, whereas others cannot. For instance, from the fact that Socrates is a man and is white it follows that he is a white man, but from the fact that he is good and is a shoemaker, it does not follow that he is a good shoemaker. Predicates that are accidental either to the same subject or to one another do not combine to form a unity.

12–14. The contradictory of 'it may be' is not 'it may not be' as it is impossible for contradictory propositions to be true of the same subject. Thus, the contradictory of 'it may be' is 'it cannot be', and the contradictory of 'it may not be' is 'it cannot not be'. Similar propositions such as 'it is necessary' and 'it is impossible' can be dealt with in a similar manner. The contradictory of 'it is necessary that it should be' is not 'it is necessary that it should not be', but 'it is not necessary that it should be', and the contradictory of 'it is necessary that it should not be' is 'it is not necessary that it should not be'. The contradictory of 'it is impossible that it should be' is not 'it is impossible that it should not be', but 'it is not possible that it should be', and the contradictory of 'it is impossible that it should not be' is 'it is not impossible that it should not be'.

CHAPTER 7

Prior Analytics

A syllogism is discourse in which, certain things
being stated, something other than what is stated
follows of necessity from their being so.

The subject of our inquiry is demonstration.

A premise or proposition is a sentence affirming or denying one thing of another; and this is either universal or particular or indefinite.

A syllogism or deduction is discourse in which, certain things being stated, something other than what is stated (the consequence) follows of necessity from their being so. A syllogism is perfect if it contains no hidden premises.

Every premise – whether affirmative or negative – states that something either is or must be or may be the attribute of something else. Some premises are universal, others particular, others indefinite. In universal attribution the terms of the negative premise are convertible, e.g. if no pleasure is good, then no good is pleasure; the terms of the affirmative premise are partly convertible, e.g. if every pleasure is good, then some good is pleasure. In particular attribution, the terms of the affirmative premise convert in part, e.g., if some pleasure is good, then some good is pleasure; however, the terms of the negative premise need not convert, e.g. if some animal is not man, it does not follow that some man is not animal.

If no B is A, then no A is B.
If every B is A, then some A is B.
If some B is A, then some A is B.
If some B is not A, it does not follow that some A are not B.

The same rules hold good in respect of necessary premises: the universal negative converts universally, each of the affirmatives converts into a particular, but the particular negative does not convert.

In respect of possible premises, affirmative statements convert in a manner similar to those described above, for if it is possible that all or some B is A, then it is possible that some A is B. Negative statements such as, 'it is possible that man is not horse' or 'it is possible that no garment is white' convert like other negative statements. However, if anything is said to be possible because it is the general rule and natural, the negative statements can no longer be converted like the simple negatives. Thus, whereas the particular negative premise converts, the universal one does not.

The statements 'it is possible that no B is A' and 'it is possible that some B is not A' is affirmative in form, as 'is possible' ranks along with 'is'. In conversions, such statements behave like any affirmative statement.

A syllogism is a three-step deductive argument containing two statements (the premises) and a third statement (the conclusion) that follows necessarily from the premises. The premise that contains the subject of the conclusion is called the minor premise, and the premise that contains the predicate of the conclusion is called the major premise. As well as three assertions, a syllogism also contains three terms. The term that is contained in the minor premise and that is the subject of the conclusion is called the minor term, and the term that is contained in the major premise and that is the predicate of the conclusion is called the major term. The remaining term is contained in both premises but not in the conclusion, and is called the middle term.

> *All men are mortal.*
> *Socrates is a man.*
> *Therefore Socrates is mortal.*

In this syllogism, the first statement is the major premise with the major term ('mortal'), and the second statement is the minor premise with the minor term ('Socrates'). The middle term is 'man'. The term 'Socrates' is particular, whereas the terms 'man' and 'mortal' are universal. 'Socrates' names one particular thing that, like many others, falls under the universals 'man' and 'mortal'. A universal term can act either as the subject or as the predicate of a statement, but a particular term can act only as the subject. Sentences that have a universal as the subject must be preceded by 'all', 'no', or 'some'. This yields four different types of 'categorical sentences', universal affirmative (a), universal negative (e), particular affirmative (i), particular negative (o).

Categorical sentence		Code Example	Shorthand
Universal affirmative	a	*All men are mortal.*	AaB
Universal negative	e	*No men are divine.*	AeB
Particular affirmative	i	*Some men are wealthy.*	AiB
Particular negative	o	*Some men are not wealthy.*	AoB

All statements can be recast into the form of one of the four categorical sentences, in which form they can be entered into syllogisms.

If S is the minor term (the subject of the conclusion), P is the major term (the predicate of the conclusion), and M is the middle term, then the major premise links M with P and the minor premise links M with S. However, M can be either the subject or the predicate of each premise. Depending on the positions of M in its major and minor premises, a syllogism can be classified into one of three 'figures'.

	Figure 1	**Figure 2**	**Figure 3**
Major premise	M–P	P–M	M–P
Minor premise	S–M	S–M	M–S
Conclusion	S–P	S–P	S–P

In the first figure the middle term is the subject of one premise and the predicate of the other, in the second figure it is the predicate of both premises, and in the third figure it is the subject of both premises. Placing each of the categorical sentences a, e, i, o into the first figure yields four valid forms of deduction.

MaP, SaM; therefore SaP
MeP, SaM; therefore SeP
MaP, SiM; therefore SiP
MeP, SiM; therefore SoP

An example of the first form is, 'All mammals are animals, all dogs are mammals; therefore all dogs are animals.' An example of the second form is, 'No mammals lay eggs, all dogs are mammals; therefore no dogs lay eggs'. An example of the third form is, 'All wines are fermented, some drinks are wine; therefore some drinks are fermented.' An example of the fourth form is, 'No wine is pasteurised; some drinks are wine; therefore, some drinks are not pasteurised.' Note that a syllogism can be described by listing the codes for the three categorical sentences. Thus, the first form is 'AAA' or 'AAA in the first figure' or 'AAA–1', the second form is 'EAE–1', and so on. Mediaeval scholars expanded these descriptions into mnemonics such as '**Barbara**' for AAA-1 and '**Celarent**' for EAE –1.

Placing each of the categorical sentences into the second figure yields four valid forms of deduction.

PeM, SaM; therefore SeP
PaM, SeM; therefore SeP
PeM, SiM; therefore SoP
PaM, SoM; therefore SoP

Placing each of the categorical sentences into the third figure yields six valid forms of deduction.

MaP, MaS; therefore SiP
MeP, MaS; therefore SoP
MiP, MaS; therefore SiP
MaP, MiS; therefore SiP
MoP, MaS; therefore SoP
MeP, Mis; therefore SoP

Note that, for a term to be interchangeable, that is, to be either in the subject or predicate position of a statement, the term must be universal or categorical. Particular terms such as 'Socrates' cannot be predicated of anything but can still appear in a syllogism if they are circumscribed to the subject position. The validity of such a non-categorical syllogism can be demonstrated by recasting it into categorical terms, with 'Socrates' becoming something like 'All that is identical to Socrates'.

CHAPTER 8

Physics

Man is begotten by man and by the sun as well.

Book 1

The *Physics* is a study of nature (*ta phusika*). As such, it treats of the natural objects that are subject to change and, more specifically, of change itself.

To know a thing, it is necessary to know its primary conditions or first principles. The first principles of nature must be either one or more than one. If one, they must be either motionless (and so changeless), as Parmenides asserts, or in motion, as the physicists assert. If more than one, they must be either finite or infinite; if infinite, they must be either one in kind or different in kind and even contrary.

Aristotle raises several arguments against the possibility that being is one and motionless. He then compares and examines the various doctrines of the presocratic natural philosophers, and concludes that, despite their differences of opinion, they all agree in identifying the first principles with contraries such as odd and even, hot and cold, and, in the case of Empedocles, love and strife. 'And with good reason,' says Aristotle, 'for first principles must not be derived from one another nor from anything else, while everything has to be derived from them.' Some of the philosophers postulate contraries that are more primary, others contraries that are less so, 'some those more knowable in the order of explanation, others those more familiar to sense.'[1]

So much is clear, that the first principles must be contraries – call them 'form' and 'privation'. While the first principles cannot be either one or innumerable, it is plausible to suppose that they are more than two, 'for Love does not gather Strife together and make things out if it, nor does Strife make anything out of Love, but both act on a third thing different from both.' This presupposes the existence of an underlying something, namely, that which becomes, or 'matter'. Although matter is numerically one, in form at least it is not one. Put differently, there is both something that comes into existence and something that becomes that. Thus, there is a sense in which the first principles are two, but, as the contraries themselves are two, there is also a sense in which they are three: matter, form, and privation. For example, a man becoming musical involves the form of musicality, the privation of unmusicality, and the underlying matter of the man who makes the change from unmusicality to musicality, with the substance involved in the change (the man) remaining constant. Some bronze becoming a statue involves the form of statue, the privation of shapelessness, and the underlying matter of the bronze which makes the change from shapelessness to statue. In the case of generation, the statue comes into existence, shapelessness ceases to exist; in that of destruction, the statue ceases to exist, shapelessness comes into existence. In both cases, the matter (the bronze) persists throughout the change.

This account of change resolves the Parmenidean dilemma according to which change is impossible because 'what is cannot come to be (since it already is), while nothing can come to be from what is not.' For Parmenides, the initial and resultant objects are simples, namely, not being and being,

1   For an outline of the thought of the presocratic philosophers, see *Plato's Shadow*.

whereas for Aristotle they are compounds, for instance, an unmusical man and a musical man. As the unmusical man is both not musical and a man, he is both not-being and being at the same time.

Notice that the case of the unmusical man becoming a musical man is a case involving the alteration of a substance, namely, man, whereas the case of the bronze becoming a statue is a case involving the transformation of matter, namely bronze, into something that has the form of a substance, namely, the statue. The first case involving the alteration of a substance is one of accidental change, whereas the second case involving the transformation of matter is one of substantial change.

Book 2

Of the things that exist, some exist by nature, some from other causes. Things that exist by nature are the animals and their parts, the plants, and the simple bodies (earth, fire, air, water), for each has within itself a principle of motion in respect of place, coming-to-be, growth, or alteration. Not so artefacts such as a bed or a coat, except coincidentally in so far as they happen to be composed of things that exist by nature. Thus, if a wooden bed were to sprout into a tree, this would not be qua bed but qua wood.

Things that exist by nature are substances, and nature is the substance or subject of a particular thing. Some say that nature resides in matter and others that it resides in form. Aristotle argues that 'man is born out of man', and thus that nature resides in form rather than in matter. However, the universe is composed of form and matter in inseparable unity throughout, and physics should concern itself with the study of both. The nature or form of a thing is also its end, but the end of a thing need not correspond to its last stage. 'For not every stage that is last claims to be an end, but only that which is best.'

Aristotle identifies four different types of causes (*aition*, cause or 'explanatory factor'): (1) the material cause, the

117

material that an object is made out of; (2) the formal cause, the form that the object takes on (conceptually expressed in its name or definition); (3) the efficient cause, the source of the change; (4) the final cause, the intended purpose of the change. For instance, a table is a flat surface on four legs (formal cause) that is made by a carpenter (efficient cause) out of wood (material cause) for the purpose of eating and writing (final cause). These four causes are illustrated in Figure 1.

Figure 1: Aristotle's four causes. Illustration by Tom Stockmann.

He rejects the notion that chance should be counted as a fifth cause. An event that occurs by chance is an event that occurs out of the coincidence of separate events each with their own separate causes; as the chance event does not have any causes of its own, it is purely incidental.

118

> *Now since nothing which is incidental is prior to*
> *what is per se, it is clear that no incidental cause*
> *can be prior to a cause per se. Spontaneity and*
> *chance, therefore, are posterior to intelligence and*
> *nature. Hence, however true it may be that the*
> *heavens are due to spontaneity, it will still be true*
> *that intelligence and nature will be prior causes of*
> *this All and of many things in it besides.*[2]

Aristotle contends that it is absurd to suppose that nature does not have a purpose, and compares nature to a doctor doctoring himself, 'the best illustration is a doctor doctoring himself: nature is like that.' Three of the four causes – the formal, efficient, and final – often coincide because in nature the formal cause is the same as the final cause, while the efficient cause or primary source of motion comes from within the object. As the end of an object necessarily implies its material cause, the material cause can also be said to be contained within the definition of the thing.

Book 3

The subject of our enquiry, namely, nature, has been defined as 'a principle of motion and change', and so it is important to enquire into the meaning of 'motion'. It is commonly held that motion belongs to the class of things that are continuous, that is, infinitely divisible, and that its necessary conditions are place, time, and void. Motion can be defined as the actuality of that which exists potentially, in so far as it is potentially this actuality. Previous accounts of motion fail to take into account that motion is an actuality. Instead, they assume that motion is indefinite because it cannot be classed simply as privation, potentiality, or actuality. According to our definition, motion is a sort of actuality, or actuality of the kind described, 'hard to grasp, but not incapable of existing'. Motion requires both the

2   Translated by RP Hardie and RK Gaye.

actuality of the agent and that of the patient, the outcome and completion of the one being an 'action' and that of the other a 'passion'. Teaching is not the same as learning, or agency as patiency, though they belong to the same subject, namely, the motion. Hence there is a single actuality of both mover and movable, 'just as one to two and two to one are the same interval, and the steep ascent and the steep descent are one – for these are one and the same, although they can be described in different ways.'

As motion requires place and time, and as both place and time are (at least potentially) infinite, it is necessary to discuss the infinite. Concerning the infinite, (*apeiron*, the unlimited), there is a sense in which it exists and another in which it does not. The infinite is an unending series of magnitudes arrived at either by addition or by division. While an infinitely large magnitude and an infinitely small magnitude can exist potentially, they cannot exist actually. Thus, there is no such thing as actual infinity (neither of magnitudes nor of bodies, substances, or voids), but only potential infinity. This solution resolves many of the contradictions and paradoxes that arise from a straight and simple affirmation or denial of the existence of infinity.

Book 4

'Motion' in its most general and primary sense is change of place or 'locomotion'. Every sensible body is in place (*topos*), and place is something distinct from body, neither a part nor a state of it. Place can be thought of as a non-portable vessel, and a vessel is not a part of the body that it contains. More precisely, place can be thought of as the innermost motionless boundary of the containing body at which it is in contact with the contained body. In short, place is a boundary or surface – not to be confused with space, which is a volume co-existent with a body. According to Aristotle's conception of the cosmos, the heaven contains concentric spheres within itself. While these concentric spheres can be said to be in heaven, heaven itself cannot be said to be contained in anything else. Hence, heaven is not in place.

Void (*kenon*) is thought to be place with nothing in it, such that where there is no body, there must be void. Given our definition of place, and given that void must, if it exists, be place deprived of body, it is plain that void does not exist. The existence of void is not only unnecessary, but leads to contradictions that make motion either unnatural or impossible. The speed of a falling object is proportional to the weight of the object, and inversely proportional to the density of the medium through which it is falling. However, in a void, all objects would fall at an infinite speed. The lighter elements of fire and air tend to rise and the heavier elements of earth and water tend to fall; these elements simply change places like bubbles of air rising through water. Similarly, with violent motions such as that of a projectile, it is the circulating material around the moving object that accounts for the object's tendency to remain in motion. Thus, a void would render all motion – whether rising or falling or horizontal as in the case of the projectile – quite impossible.

> *In time all things come into being and pass away;*
> *for which reason some called it the wisest of all*
> *things, but the Pythagorean Paron called it the*
> *most stupid, because in it we also forget; and his*
> *was the truer view.*

Time (*chronos*) consists of a part that has been and is not, and another that is going to be and is not yet. Something that is made up of things that do not exist can have no share in reality. 'Now' is not a part of time, for time is not held to be made up of 'nows'. Time is often thought of in terms of motion and thus in terms of a kind of change, but motion is only ever in the thing that moves. Moreover, motion can be said to be defined by time in that it can be faster or slower, but time cannot be said to be defined by time. Clearly then, time cannot be thought of in terms of motion or change. However, without motion 'now' would be one and the same and time could not be said to exist. Thus, time is neither motion nor independent of motion. Aristotle concludes that time is the numerical aspect of motion, and defines it as 'number of movement in respect to the before and after'. However, there are not a series of 'nows', but only one 'now' that is associated with different events and that thereby produces the experience of before and after. This 'now' (the present) is the extremity of past and future, the shared and indivisible limit of both. To exist, time requires soul or mind to number its movement. Without soul, there would not be time but only that of which time is an attribute, namely, motion. The best motion with which to mark time is both uniform and circular, which explains why time is marked by the daily motion of the heavens.

Books 5 & 6
Every motion is a kind of change. Of the three possible kinds of change, those which imply a relation of contradiction, namely becoming ('generation') and perishing ('corruption'), are not motions. Thus, the only motion is change from subject to subject. Every subject is either a contrary or an intermediate and can be affirmatively expressed as e.g. naked, toothless, or black. Of the ten categories, change can only take place in respect of quality (alteration), quantity (increase or decrease), and location (locomotion). As change is not a substance, it does not itself admit of properties, and therefore does not itself admit of change. The opposite of a change is not another change, but rest.

Aristotle presents a series of logical arguments to demonstrate that anything that is continuous cannot be composed of indivisibles, for instance, a line cannot be composed of points, since a line is continuous but a point is indivisible. Thus, everything that is continuous is divisible into divisibles that are infinitely divisible. The same reasoning applies equally to magnitude, to time, and to motion. Building

Figure 2: The dichotomy paradox. According to Zeno, an object in locomotion must arrive at the half-way stage before it can arrive at the goal, but to arrive at this half-way stage it must first arrive at another half-way stage (the quarter-way stage), and so on infinitely, such that it can never even get started. Illustration by Tom Stockmann.

upon this, Aristotle proposes to resolve Zeno's four paradoxes of motion, which purport to demonstrate that motion – and by extension change – cannot exist. For instance, the dichotomy paradox asserts the non-existence of motion on the ground that an object in locomotion must arrive at the half-way stage before it can arrive at the goal, and that to arrive at this half-way stage it must first arrive at another half-way stage (the quarter-way stage), and so on infinitely, such that it can never even get started. Aristotle's solution to the dichotomy paradox, which is illustrated in Figure 2, is that time can be divided just as infinitely as space, and thus that it would take an infinitely small amount of time to cover the infinitely small amount of space required for the object to get started. The Achilles paradox asserts that, in a race, the quickest runner can never overtake the slowest, since the quickest must first reach the point at which the slowest started, and so on to infinity. The Achilles paradox is the same in principal as the dichotomy paradox (except that the successive spaces do not divide into halves), and so too the solution must be the same. In essence, Zeno assumes that the infinity of points that separate the quickest from the slowest runner is an actual infinity when it is in fact only a potential infinity.

Books 7 & 8

Everything that is in motion must be moved by something else. A thing that is in motion is moved by something else that is in motion, which is itself moved by something else that is in motion, and that by something else, and so on; as this series cannot go on to infinity, there must exist some prime mover. Since there are three kinds of motion, local, qualitative, and quantitative, there must also be three kinds of prime mover, that which causes locomotion, that which causes alteration, and that which causes increase or decrease. Let us begin with the primary motion, namely, locomotion. Everything that is in locomotion is moved either by itself or by something else. Things that are moved by themselves contain their prime mover within themselves. Things that are moved by something else must proceed in one of four ways: pulling, pushing, carrying, and rotating. Carrying always follows one of the other three methods (for that which is carried is upon something that is in motion) and rotating is a compound of pulling and pushing. As it is impossible to move anything without being in contact with it, it is evident that in all locomotion there cannot be anything intermediate between mover and moved. Nor can there be anything intermediate between that which undergoes and that which causes alteration, increase, or decrease. The distance that an object moves in a certain time is related to the ratio of the force (the mover) to the moved object. If a force F moves an object A along a distance d in a time t, then half F moves half A along the same distance in the same time. The relationship need not be proportional, however, or else a single man could move a large ship if only he kept at it for long enough.

It remains to consider whether or not motion is eternal. If there ever has been a time without motion, this would have been either because all things were together and at rest before the introduction of motion (as Anaxagoras purports), or because the universe is alternatively at rest and in motion (as Empedocles purports). However, any motion needs an earlier cause, and time cannot exist without motion. Therefore, motion is eternal. Against this it might be argued that: (1) change proceeds from one thing to another, such that change must be finite; (2) inanimate things that are at rest can be set into motion, such that there can be a becoming of motion; (3) animate beings can spontaneously set themselves in motion, and if this is true of the animal then it might also be true of the universe as a whole. In response to these arguments it may be said to (1) that there is no reason why change cannot be infinite; to (2) that the change in inanimate things occurs from without; and to (3) that animate beings are never truly at rest, and that many of their motions are actually produced from without. The real question at issue here is this: why some things are at one time in motion and at another at rest? Either (1) all things are always at rest, or (2) all things are always in motion, or (3) some things are at rest and others in motion. In this last case, either (1) the things that are at rest are always at rest and the things that are in motion are always in motion, or (2) both are capable of both rest and motion, or (3) some things are always at rest, others always in motion, and others still are capable of both rest and motion. It is possible to reject all these possibilities except the last on the grounds of our sense perception that some things are sometimes in motion and at other times at rest. Thus, the last is the account of the matter that must be given, for in it is the solution to all the difficulties raised and the conclusion of our investigation. It remains to consider whether all things are capable of both rest and motion, or whether, while only some things are capable of both rest and motion, some others are always at rest and some others are always in motion. Some things are moved by an eternal unmoved mover and are therefore always in motion, but other things are moved by a mover that is in motion and changing, so that they too must change. Therefore, there must be things that are sometimes in motion and sometimes not. The unmoved mover is not only eternal but also unchanging, indivisible, without parts, and without magnitude. The primary kind of change is movement, and the primary kind of movement is circular movement. The prime mover causes the circular movement of the heavens which in turn causes all other movements in the sublunary world.

CHAPTER 9

On the Heavens

It may seem evidence of excessive folly or excessive zeal to try to provide an explanation of some things, or of everything, admitting no exception.

Book 1

Of things constituted by nature some are bodies and magnitudes, some possess body and magnitude, and some are principles of things which possess these. A continuum is that which is infinitely divisible, and a body is that which is in every way divisible. A magnitude if divisible one way is a line, if two ways a surface, if three ways a body. Beyond these there is no other magnitude, because the three dimensions are all that there are, and that which is divisible in three directions is divisible in all.

> *For, as the Pythagoreans say, the world and all that is in it is determined by the number three, since beginning and middle and end give the number of an 'all', and the number they give is the triad. And so, having taken these three from nature as (so to speak) laws of it, we make further use of the number three in the worship of the Gods.*[1]

1   Translated by JL Stocks.

Thus, body alone among magnitudes can be complete, for it alone is determined by all three dimensions, that is, is an 'all'. Bodies which are parts of the whole are complete, even though each is determined in relation to that part which is next to it by contact, for which reason each is in a sense many bodies. But the whole of which they are parts must necessarily be complete and thus have being, not in some respect only but in every respect.

All natural bodies and magnitudes are capable of locomotion, and all locomotion is either straight or circular or a combination of the two. Circular locomotion is revolution about the centre, and straight locomotion is either upward, away from the centre, or downward, towards the centre. Just as body found its completion in three dimensions, so its movement completes itself in three forms.

Simple bodies have a simple movement, either upward, as in the case of fire and air, or downward, as in the case of earth and water. However, there are also simple bodies that move in a circle, implying that there must be some other element, ether, with a circular motion. As the circle is perfect, and as the perfect is naturally prior to the imperfect, circular motion is necessarily primary. Thus, ether, the substance of circular motion, is both prior to and more divine than the other elements. As ether neither moves upwards, away from the centre of its circular motion, or downwards, towards the centre of its circular motion, it cannot possess either lightness or heaviness. As there can be no contrary motion to the circular (for circular motion from B to A is not the contrary of circular motion from A to B), ether cannot have contraries, and it is therefore reasonable to assume that it is ungenerated and indestructible and exempt from increase, decrease, and alteration. This explains why the heavens appear to be eternal and unchanging.

Is there an infinite body? A body is necessarily either simple or composite. If simple bodies are finite, then composite bodies (which are made out of simple bodies) must also be finite. So can a simple body be infinite? The simple body that moves in a circle must necessarily be finite because, if not, the radii drawn from the centre will be infinite, in which case the space between the radii will also be infinite and hence could not be traversed in circular motion. Aristotle marshals up six other arguments to demonstrate the impossibility of circular motion in a simple body that is infinite. He then proceeds to demonstrate the impossibility of rectilinear motion in a simple body that is infinite. As the upward and downward motions are contraries, they must be towards contrary places, and if one of a pair of contraries is determinate (and the centre is determined), then the other must be determinate also. From this alone it is clear that an infinite body is impossible. But there is also something else. Given that a body moves a distance in a time that is inversely proportional to its weight, a body that is infinitely heavy would take no time at all to move, whereas a body that is infinitely light would take forever. An infinite body would have to be either infinitely heavy or infinitely light; neither is possible, and so nor is an infinite body. Aristotle sets out a number of other more or less intricate arguments to demonstrate the impossibility of an infinite body.

Even though there cannot be an infinite body, there might yet be more than one world. Since the movements in another world would be the same, so would the elements, such that particles of earth would move naturally to the centre and particles of fire to the extremity. This, however, is impossible, since earth would then move to the extremity and fire to the centre, just as earth in our world that moved to the centre of another world would move to the extremity of ours, and fire in our world that moved to the periphery of another world would move to the centre of ours. Therefore, there can only be one centre, one extremity, and one world. As that which is moved changes from one thing to its contrary, the starting point and the goal of natural movement must differ in form. So, too, earth and fire must move not to infinity but to opposite points, namely, the centre and the periphery.

Just as there are three elements, so there are three places for the elements: the centre for heavy objects; the outermost place for the weightless, revolving ether; and the intermediate place for the light element.

One might think that it is impossible for there to be no more than one world, since in all formations whether of nature or of art one is able to distinguish both the shape in itself (form) and that shape in combination with matter (form in matter, i.e. a particular). Since the universe is perceptible, it must be regarded as a particular, and any particular has, or may have, more than one instance. However, a plurality of worlds is impossible if this world contains the entirety of matter, as in fact it does. Indeed, the whole included within the extreme circumference must be composed of all physical and sensible body because there cannot be any body outside the heaven: the proper places of each element have been defined, and neither place is nor can be outside the heaven. It is therefore evident that there is also no place or void or time outside the heaven, and that whatever there might be is of such a nature as not to occupy any place, nor to be affected by time, nor to be subject to motion and change.

Is the heaven generated or ungenerated, destructible or indestructible? Some think it possible for the ungenerated to be destroyed and for the generated to persist undestroyed, but both are in fact impossible. It is impossible for the ungenerated to be destroyed because a thing which had no beginning contains no cause or capacity for change. And it is impossible for the generated to persist undestroyed because things that are seen to be generated are also seen to be destroyed. That which is eternal can neither be generated nor destroyed; conversely, that which is generated or destructible cannot be eternal.

Book 2

Our notion is that the world is neither generated nor destructible, but that it is eternal without either beginning or end. 'Hence it is well to persuade oneself of the truth of the ancient and truly traditional theories, that there is some immortal and divine thing which possesses movement, but movement such as has no limit and is rather itself the limit of all other movement.' The ancients gave to the gods the upper place, as being alone immortal, and our present argument testifies that the upper place is ungenerated and indestructible. Moreover, as the heaven is perfect, it is effortless, and needs no Atlas to hold it up.

It has already been determined that functions such as above and below, right and left belong to things that have a principle of movement, and that the heaven is animate and possesses a principle of movement. Clearly, the heaven must also exhibit above and below, right and left, even though it is spherical in shape and all its parts are alike and for ever in motion. Even if the heaven never began to move, yet it must possess a principle from which it would have begun to move if it had begun. Right in anything is the region in which locomotion originates, and the rotation of the heaven originates in the region from which the stars rise. So this is the right, and the region where the stars set is the left. If then the stars begin from the right and move round to the right, the pole which we see above us is the lower pole, and that which we do not see is the upper pole. Those who live in the other hemisphere are above and to the right, while we are below and to the left. However, relative to the secondary revolution, that is, the revolution of the planets, we are above and to the right and they are below and to the left. For the principle of their movement has the reverse position, since the movement itself is the contrary of the other.

As reverse circular motion is not the contrary of circular motion, it is necessary to ask why there is more than one heavenly motion. There must be something at rest at the centre of the revolving body, namely, earth, and if earth must exist, so must its contrary, namely, fire, and so must the intermediate bodies. As they are contraries, these four elements cannot be eternal, and so must be generated. But if they are generated, there must be at least one other circular motion, for a single movement of the whole heaven would necessitate an identical relation of the elements of bodies to one another.

The shape of the heaven is of necessity spherical, for that is the shape most appropriate to its substance and also by nature primary. Just as the circle is primary among figures, so the sphere is primary among solids, for it alone is embraced by a single surface. Aristotle presents a number of other arguments to demonstrate that the shape of the heaven is of necessity spherical.

Why does the circular motion of the heaven take one direction rather than the other? Either this is an ultimate fact or there is an ultimate fact behind it. Nature always follows the best course possible, and, just as upward movement is the superior form of rectilinear movement, since the upper region is more divine than the lower, so circular movement to the right may be the superior form of circular movement.

> *It may seem evidence of excessive folly or excessive zeal to try to provide an explanation of some things, or of everything, admitting no exception. The criticism, however, is not always just: one should first consider what reason there is for speaking, and also what kind of certainty is looked for, whether human merely or of a more cogent kind. When any one shall succeed in finding proofs of greater precision, gratitude will be due to him for the discovery, but at present we must be content with a probable solution.*

Is the movement of the heaven regular or irregular? If the movement were irregular, this would necessarily imply acceleration, maximum speed, and deceleration. The maximum may occur either at the starting point (as with unnatural motion) or at the goal (as with natural motion) or somewhere inbetween (as with projectile motion). But as circular movement has no beginning or end or middle, it cannot admit of a maximum, and so must be regular. Furthermore, since everything that is moved is moved by something, the cause of the irregularity of movement would have to lie either in the mover or in the moved or in both. However, both the mover and the moved are primary and simple and ungenerated and indestructible and generally unchanging. And there are also other arguments against the irregular movement of the heaven, for instance, that the stars have never been observed to move relative to one another.

The stars, being in heaven, are composed of ether, but appear fiery because of the friction produced by their motion. Changes evidently occur not only in the position of the stars but also in that of the whole heaven. Since it is unreasonable to suppose that both are in motion or that the stars alone are in motion, the remaining alternative is that the circles should move, while the stars are at rest and move with the circles to which they are attached. The spherical body has two movements proper to itself, namely, rolling and spinning, but in the stars neither is observed. If the stars spun, they would not change their place, which they do. And if they rolled, the moon would not always present the same unchanging face, which it does. If the stars appear to twinkle, this is not because they are spinning, but because the prolonged distance that separates them from the earth causes their rays to be weak. On the other hand, the planets are much closer to the earth, and so do not appear to twinkle. From all this, it is clear that the theory of the Pythagoreans according to which the movement of the stars produces a harmony is false, since there do not seem to be any effects of such a sound, neither the sound itself, nor any effects of the sound (for example, excessive noises can shatter solid bodies). Bodies which are themselves in motion do produce noise and friction, but those that are fixed to a moving body do not. Furthermore, a moving body only produces sound if it is enclosed in an unmoved body, and not if it is enclosed in, and continuous with, a moving body which creates no friction.

Why is there the greatest number of movements in the intermediate bodies, rather than, in each successive body, a movement proportionate to its distance from the primary motion? Indeed, the movements of the sun and the moon are fewer than those of some of the planets. Yet these planets are further from the centre and thus nearer to the primary body than both the sun and the moon. As the planets are closer to earth than the stars, their action is similar to that of animated beings. Just as man has a multiplicity of movements, so do the planets that are closest to Earth. However, the Earth itself is motionless, and the planets that are closest to it, the sun and the moon, are only capable of a simple movement. Why is it that the primary motion includes such a great multitude of stars, while the planets with special motions are so few in number? This arrangement is a natural one, as the first heaven is far superior to the others. Nature makes matters equal and establishes a certain order, giving to the single movement many bodies and to the single body many movements.

Some people, such as the Pythagoreans, hold that it is not earth but fire that is at the centre of the sphere, and that the earth revolves about the centre. With regards to the shape of the earth, some think it spherical, others flat and drum-shaped. Many are puzzled that a handful of earth let loose in mid-air starts to fall, whereas the earth itself, which is far heavier, can hang and hold still in the centre of the sphere. 'The difficulty then, has naturally passed into a common place of philosophy; and one may well wonder that the solutions offered are not seen to involve greater absurdities than the problem itself.' Thus, some have asserted, along with Xenophanes of Colophon, that the earth below us is infinite. Others have asserted, along with Thales of Miletus, that the earth rests upon water. According to Anaximenes and Anaxagoras and Democritus, the earth stays still because it is flat and supported by confined air. Empedocles says that it came together and is maintained at the centre because of the whirl of the heavens. And Anaximander that it keeps its place because of its indifference. Aristotle rebuts each of these claims. If the earth did have a natural movement around the sun or some other centre, then every part of it would have this movement, when in fact every part of it moves in a straight line to centre. Thus, if the earth did move around the sun or some other centre, this movement would have to be constrained and unnatural, and so could not be eternal. Also, the stars would appear to rise and to set in different places, even though no such thing is observed. From these considerations it is clear that the earth lies at the centre and does not move.

As every portion of earth naturally moves to the centre, the shape of the earth must necessarily be spherical. Indeed, the outline of the earth seen in eclipses of the moon is curved, and some stars that are seen in Cyprus or Egypt are not seen in northerly regions. The latter indicates not only that the earth is a sphere, but also that it is of no great size, and one should not be too surprised if the ocean that lies beyond the pillars of Heracles is the same as that of the Indians. Indeed, elephants are found in both Libya and India, and some mathematicians have calculated the size of the earth's circumference at 400,000 stadia.

Book 3

Having spoken of the primary element and of its freedom from generation and destruction, it remains to speak of the other two elements. However, in so doing, it will be necessary also to inquire into generation and destruction. Melissus and Parmenides maintain that generation and destruction are merely an illusion, and others are of the contrary opinion, with some maintaining even that nothing is ungenerated. The theory that generation involves the composition and separation of planes is false, for if solids are composed of planes, and planes of lines, and lines of points, then a part of a line need not be a line, and the line is therefore indivisible. Many attributes that are present in physical bodies are necessarily excluded by such indivisibility. For instance, if the point, by virtue of being indivisible, has no weight, then neither does the line, the plane, or indeed the body.

Each of the simple bodies manifestly moves, and if they have no natural movement then they must move by constraint or unnaturally. However, an unnatural movement presupposes a natural movement which it contravenes and which, however many the unnatural movements, is always one. Rest also must be natural or constrained, natural in a place movement to which is natural, or constrained in a place movement to which is constrained. There is manifestly a body at rest at the centre, and if this place of rest is natural to it, then movement to this place is also natural to it. If, on the other hand, its rest is constrained, what is hindering its motion? Its motion could not be hindered by something that is itself at rest, or else there is an infinite regress. And if its motion is hindered by something that is in motion, where would it have moved to had it not been for that moving thing? It could not move infinitely, for that is impossible, and so it would have to stop at some place where it would rest naturally. And if it has some place in which it could rest naturally, then it must also have a natural movement to that place of rest. Disorder should not be confused with diversity of directions in motion, which is a species of order. If disorder had been the norm, no natural fact, such as animals composed of flesh and bone, could possibly have come into existence. Thus, every body has its natural movement, and this natural movement finds its impetus in the body's weight or lightness. A weightless object could not move naturally, as things fall faster the heavier they are, and rise faster the lighter they are.

It is quite possible for one body to be generated out of another, for instance, air out of fire, but in the absence of any pre-existing mass generation is impossible. This is because the place that would be occupied by a thing that was being generated *ex nihilo* would have had to be occupied by extracorporeal void, which is impossible. An element is a body into which other bodies may be analysed, present in them potentially or in actuality, and not itself divisible into bodies different in form. For instance, fire and earth can be extruded from wood, but wood cannot be extruded from either element. If body is distinguished from body by the appropriate qualitative difference, and if there is a limit to the number of such differences, then there must also be a limit to the number of elements. Again, if every element has its proper movement, and if there is a limit to the number of simple movements, then there must also be a limit to the number of elements. It is clear, therefore, that the number of elements is limited. Some assume that there is only one element, variously water, air, fire, or an infinite body. If this were the case, then there would be only one simple movement, which is clearly not the case. The elements undergo a process of analysis. If this process of analysis continued infinitely, the opposite process of synthesis would also have to continue infinitely, which is impossible. Thus, the process of analysis must stop somewhere, and the reason that it stops somewhere is that there is no longer any element left to change. This implies not only that one element can be changed into another, but also that the elements are subject to destruction and generation. The elements cannot be generated from something incorporeal, since that would require an extra-corporeal void. Nor can they be generated from some kind of body, since that would involve a body distinct from the elements and prior to them. The only remaining alternative is that they are generated from one another. How so? Not by being excreted from one another, as some maintain, but by changing into one another. As there are only three plane figures that can fill a space, the triangle, the square, and the hexagon, and only two solids, the pyramid and the cube, the elements cannot each have a different shape. Again, the elements often take the shape of their container and combine with each other to form composites such as flesh and bone, which they could not do if they each had a different shape.

Book 4

How then can the different functions, properties, and powers of the elements be explained? Heavy and light can be either relative or absolute, relative in that, say, wood is heavier than bronze, and absolute in that the natural movement of heavy things is downward (to the centre) and the natural movement of lights things is upward (to the extremity). Some say that a thing is heavy or light because it has a greater or lesser number of identical parts, but this says nothing of the absolutely heavy and light, for fire always moves upwards, and a greater quantity of fire moves upwards faster than a lesser quantity. Others say that a thing is heavy or light because it contains a lesser or greater amount of void, and fire is the lightest of things because it has the most void. However, this does not explain why a great amount of fire moves upwards when a small amount of earth moves downwards, even though the substance in the great amount of fire is heavier than that in the small amount of earth.

Fire is absolutely light in that it always moves upwards and earth is absolutely heavy in that it always moves downwards. Air and water are relatively heavier than fire and relatively lighter than earth, but, compared together, air is absolutely light and water is absolutely heavy, since, regardless of quantity, air always rises to the surface of water and water always sinks to the bottom of air. A talent's weight of wood is heavier than a mina of lead in air but not in water, the reason being that wood contains more air than lead, and so finds its rightful place between air and water. Fire has no weight and earth no lightness as the one moves to the centre and the other to the extremity. Air and water have both lightness and weight, and water sinks to the bottom of all things except earth, while air rises to the surface of all things except fire. Since there is one body which rises to the surface of all things

138

and one which sinks to the bottom of all things, there needs to be two other bodies which sink in some bodies and rise to the surface of others. The kinds of matter, then, must be as numerous as these bodies, that is, four. A flat piece of metal floats upon water because water is harder to cleave than air, and a flat object is poorly designed to cleave through water and to begin falling.

CHAPTER 10

On the Soul

*...thinking has more resemblance to a coming to
rest or arrest than to a movement.*

Book 1

The soul is the principle of animal life, and knowledge of it
contributes greatly to our understanding of nature and of the
truth in general. What is the essential nature of the soul, and
what are its properties? To reply to these questions with any
degree of certainty is one of the most difficult things in the
world.

According to our predecessors, the chief characteristics
of an ensouled body and therefore of soul are movement and
sensation. Democritus said that soul is a sort of fire or hot
substance, and that it consists of spherical atoms that set
the other types of atom in movement by being themselves
in movement, like the motes in a sunbeam. He regards
respiration as the characteristic mark of life because it enables
spherical atoms to enter the body and thereby to counteract
the compressing force of the environment and prevent the
extrusion of those spherical atoms that are already within the
body. The Pythagoreans also declare the motes, or that which
moves them, to be soul, and similar opinions are shared by
all those who define soul as that which moves itself and by

which everything else is moved. Thales holds that the magnet has soul in it because it moves iron, and Alcmaeon that soul is immortal because it resembles the divine planets in their perpetual motion. Democritus does not distinguish soul and mind, but Anaxagoras says that not all animals have mind and not even all human beings. At the same time, he affirms that it is mind that set the whole into movement. Those who define soul less in terms of movement and more in terms of knowledge and perception identify soul with the principle or principles of nature. Thus, Empedocles said that soul is formed out of all of his elements, for like is known by like (it is by earth that earth is seen, and so on), and Plato also fashions soul out of his elements. Some, accepting the premises that the chief characteristics of soul are movement and cognition, have compounded soul of both and declared it to be a self-moving number. Reasoning that the originator of movement must be primordial, some regard soul as fire because it is the most subtle and incorporeal of elements and both moves and originates movement. Others, including Diogenes, regard soul as air because it is the finest in grain of the elements and a first principle. Anaxagoras is alone in saying that soul has nothing in common with anything else, but then fails to explain how, or in virtue of what, it is able to know.

There is no necessity that the originator of movement should itself be moved. A thing can be moved either directly, owing to itself, or indirectly, owing to something other than itself. A thing is indirectly moved if it is contained in something that is itself moved, for instance, a sailor in a ship is indirectly moved. Is the soul moved directly or indirectly? There are four species of movement by which the soul might be directly moved, locomotion, alteration, increase and decrease, and growth. All four species of movement involve place, so if soul has a natural movement, then place must be natural to it. Also, if soul has a natural movement, it must have a counter-movement that is unnatural to it, and the same applies to its natural place of rest. However, it is senseless to speak of enforced movements or rests of the soul. If the natural movement of the soul is upward, the soul must be fire, if downward, it must be earth, and so on. Furthermore, since the soul is observed to originate movement in the body, it would be reasonable to suppose that it transmits to the body the movements by which it is itself moved. As the body moves from place to place by locomotion, it would follow that the soul does so as well, in which case it might even quit and re-enter its body. As an animal can be pushed out of its course, so the soul can be moved indirectly by something else, whereas a thing that is moved by itself cannot be moved by something else except incidentally. Democritus and others maintain that the movements which the soul imparts to the body are the same in kind as those with which it is itself moved. If the ceaselessly moving spherical atoms of Democritus do indeed produce the body's movements, how could they also produce the body's rest? Moreover, the soul does not appear to originate movement in this manner, but through intention or process of thinking. In the *Timaeus*, Plato says that the soul moves the body by their mutual implication, and suggests that the soul is a spatial magnitude that moves in an eternal circular motion. However, if mind has a unity, then it is not a unity like that of spatial magnitude, but a serial unity like that of number. And if the circular motion is eternal, then what is it that mind is endlessly and repeatedly thinking? Furthermore, thinking has more resemblance to a coming to rest or arrest than to a movement. And there are other problems too. In short, the problem with this and most theories about the soul is that they join the soul to a body, or place it in a body, without adequately or at all explaining the why or how of this union.

Another theory about the soul is that it is a kind of harmony in the sense that the body is compounded of contraries and a harmony is a composition of contraries. However, soul can be neither the one nor the other of these contraries, nor can the origination of movement belong to a harmony. Thus, the soul cannot be a harmony or be moved in a circle, but it can be moved incidentally, and it can be moved indirectly as a sailor in a ship. In no other sense can the soul be moved in space. The soul may be said to be pained or pleased, bold or fearful, angry, perceiving, and thinking. These all are regarded as modes of movement, but it does not necessarily follow that it is the soul, rather than the man, that is moved. Movement may sometimes start in the soul or terminate in the soul, and yet not reside in the soul. The case of mind, however, is different. Mind seems to be an independent substance implanted within the soul and incapable of being destroyed. Indeed, the incapacity of old age is due not to an affection of the soul, but to an affection of the body, as occurs in drunkenness or disease. Thinking, loving, and hating are affections not of mind but of body, and go out as the body decays.

> *Thinking, loving, and hating are affections not of mind, but of that which has mind, so far as it has it. That is why, when this vehicle decays, memory and love cease; they were activities not of mind, but of the composite which has perished; mind is, no doubt, something more divine and impassable.*[1]

That the soul cannot be moved has become quite clear, and if it cannot be moved at all, then it cannot be moved by itself. Of all the opinions so far, by far the most unreasonable is that which declares the soul to be a self-moving number. Not only does it involve all the impossibilities which follow from regarding the soul as being moved, but also those special absurdities that follow from calling it a number. The view is identical with that of those who maintain that soul is a subtle kind of body. If the soul is present throughout the body, then this implies that there are two bodies in the same place or many points at one point, and that the body must be moved by its number just as Democritus explained it to be moved by spherical psychic

1   Translated by JA Smith.

atoms. It follows that both movement and number cannot be attributes of soul.

It remains to examine the doctrine that soul is composed of the elements. Its proponents assume that like is known only by like, but the soul apprehends not just the elements but also composite wholes such as man and bone which could not enter into the constitution of the soul. The same applies to concepts such as 'the good' and 'the not-good'. And there are many other problems too.

The functions of (a) knowing, perceiving, and opining, and (b) desiring, wishing, and other appetitive functions belong to soul, and (c) the local movements of animals, and (d) growth and decay are produced by the soul. Is each of these an attribute of the soul as a whole, or does each require a different part of the soul? So too with regard to life: does life depend on one, or more than one, or all of the parts of soul? Or does it have some quite other cause? If the soul admits of being divided, what can it be that holds its parts together? Whatever it is surely has the best right to the name soul, and so on to infinity. And if the soul admits of being divided, what is the separate role of each part in relation to the body? Plants and certain insects go on living when divided into segments, suggesting that each of the segments has a soul in it identical in species, though not numerically identical in the different segments. This implies that, although the whole soul is divisible, its several parts cannot be severed from one another.

Book 2

So much for historical accounts of the soul: let us dismiss them and make a fresh start. 'Substance' refers to (a) matter, as in potentiality, (b) form or essence, as in actuality, (c) that which is compounded of both matter and form. Among substances are bodies and especially natural bodies. Of natural bodies, some have life in them, others not, and every natural body that has life is necessarily a substance in the sense of being a composite. However, the body is the subject or matter, not that which is attributed to it. Hence, the soul must be a substance in the sense of the form of a natural body having life potentially within it. As substance is actuality, soul is the actuality (*entelecheia*) of a body, that in virtue of which it is the kind of body that it is. There are two kinds or grades of actuality, one that is akin to the possession of knowledge, and another to the exercise of knowledge. The first grade of actuality is thus a capacity to engage in the activity which is the corresponding second grade of actuality, and soul can be thought of as such a capacity, namely, a capacity to engage in the sorts of activity that are characteristic of the natural body of which it is the form, for instance, self-nourishment, growth, decay, movement and rest, perception, and intellect. Thus, the soul can be described as the first grade of actuality of a natural organised body.

> *That is why we can wholly dismiss as unnecessary the question whether the soul and the body are one: it is as meaningless as to ask whether the wax and the shape given to it by the stamp are one, or generally the matter of a thing and that of which it is the matter. Unity has many senses (as many as 'is' has), but the most proper and fundamental sense of both is the relation of an actuality to that of which it is the actuality ... [The soul] is a substance in the sense which corresponds to the definitive formula of a thing's essence.*

From this, it is evident that the soul is inseparable from its body. Yet, if the soul has parts, some of its parts may be separable because they are not actualities of any body at all.

The capacity for self-nutrition can be isolated from the other capacities mentioned, but not they from it. Self-nutrition is the originative power the possession of which is the *sine qua non* of life. Indeed, it is the only psychic power that plants possess; for a living object to be an animal, it must possess sensation as well, even though it may not possess power of local movement. The primary form of sensation is touch, which belongs to all animals, and just like self-nutrition can be isolated from touch and sensation generally, so touch can be isolated from all other forms of sensation. Is each of these capacities a soul or a part of a soul? Plants can be divided and continue to live, indicating that the soul of each individual plant before division is actually one, potentially many. The same is true also of insects that have been bisected, with each segment possessing both sensation and local movement, and, if sensation, necessarily also imagination and appetite, for where there is sensation, there is also pleasure and pain, and where these necessarily also desire. But what about the power for thought or mind, which seems to be possessed by man only? Mind seems to be a widely different kind of soul, differing as that which is eternal from that which is perishable, and alone capable of existence in isolation from all other psychic powers.

The power for self-nutrition is the most primitive and widely distributed power of the soul, and is the one in virtue of which living things are said to have life. The acts in which it manifests itself are the use of food and reproduction – reproduction so that, in as far as its nature allows, a living body may partake in the eternal and divine, which is the goal towards which all things strive. The soul is the cause or source of the living body in the sense that it is (a) the source or origin of movement (whether local movement or change in quality – as in sensation – and change in quantity – as in growth and decay), (b) the end, (c) the essence of the living body. It is manifest that the soul is also the final cause of its body. Nothing except that which is alive can be fed, such that that which is fed is the besouled body, fed by virtue of being besouled. Food not only increases the quantity of that which is fed and assists in its reproduction, but also maintains its being. This is why, if deprived of food, it must cease to be. All food must be capable of being digested. That which produces digestion is warmth, which is why every body that possesses a soul also possesses warmth.

Sensation depends on a process of movement or affection from without, for it is held to be some sort of change of quality. That which is sensitive is so only potentially, not actually, which is why the senses themselves are not perceived, or why they do not produce sensation without the stimulation of external objects. It is possible to distinguish not only between potential and actual, but also between different senses in which things can be said to be potential or actual. That which in the case of knowing leads from potential to actual ought not to be called teaching but something else. That with the potential for knowing ought not to be said 'to be acted upon', or else there are two senses of alteration, (a) the substitution of one quality for another, the first being the contrary of the second, or (b) the development of an existent quality from potentiality in the direction of fixity or nature. In the case of that with the potential for sensation, the first transition is due to the action of the male parent and occurs before birth such that, at birth, the living thing is, with respect to sensation, at the stage which corresponds to the possession of knowledge. The exercise of sensation, that is, actual sensation, corresponds with the exercise of knowledge. However, the objects that provoke actual sensation are outside, for actual sensation apprehends individuals, whereas knowledge apprehends universals, and these are in a sense within the soul. This explains why a person can exercise his knowledge at any time, but not his sensation. A similar statement can be made about knowledge of sensible objects which are individual and external.

The term 'object of sense' covers three kinds of objects, two of which are directly perceptible, while the remaining one is only incidentally perceptible. Of the first two kinds, one consists of that which is perceptible by a single sense (for instance, colour, sound, flavour, which are special objects of some sense) and the other of that which is perceptible by any and all of the senses (for instance, movement, number, figure, magnitude). Properly speaking, it is the special objects of the several senses that are objects of sense, for it is to them that the structure of each sense is specially adapted. An incidental object of sense is one where, for example, the white object that is seen is the son of Diares; the son of Diares is only incidentally perceived because 'being the son of Diares' is only incidental to the patch of white.

That which is visible is colour, which lies upon the object of sight. Every colour has in it the power to set in movement that which is transparent, which explains why colour is not visible except with the help of light. By 'transparent' is meant that which is visible, and yet not visible in itself, but owing to the colour of something else, for instance, air, water, and many solid bodies. The activity of that which is transparent is light, and light is, as it were, the proper colour of that which is transparent. Light is brought about if the potentially transparent is excited to actuality by the influence of fire or something resembling the uppermost body. Light is neither fire nor any kind of body or efflux from any kind of body, but the presence of fire or something resembling fire in that which is transparent. Light is certainly not a body, for two bodies cannot be present in the same place. That which is capable of taking on colour is that which is colourless, namely, that which is transparent or that which is invisible or dark. That which is invisible or dark is in fact that which is transparent, but only potentially rather than actually. There are some things that are invisible in light but that are fiery or shining in darkness, such as fungi, flesh, heads, scales, and eyes of fish. However, that which is seen is not their proper colour, for without light colour remains invisible. If that which has colour is placed in immediate contact with the eye, it cannot be seen, for colour sets in movement not the sense organ but that which is transparent, and it is only this that can set the sense organ in movement. The same account holds also of sound and smell and even, in spite of all appearances, of touch and taste. Only fire can be seen both in light and darkness, for only fire can make that which is potentially transparent actually transparent.

Some things such as sponges cannot make a sound and others such as bronze and in general all things that are smooth and solid can. Actual sound requires two such bodies and a space between them, for that which sounds does so by striking against something else, and this is impossible without a movement from place to place. What is required is an impact of two solids against one another and against the air. This latter condition is satisfied only if the air impinged is not dispersed by the blow, which is why the blow should be sudden and sharp. The air in the ear is built into a chamber just so as to prevent such dispersion. Voice is a kind of sound characteristic of that which has soul in it. Nature employs breath both to regulate the inner temperature of the body and to articulate voice, although the latter function is a luxury that is not found in all animals. Voice is the impact of inbreathed air against the windpipe. That which produces the impact must have soul in it and must be accompanied by an act of imagination, for voice is a sound with a meaning, and not merely any impact of the breath such as a grunt or a cough. If fish are without voice, this is because they do not breathe or take in air and so do not have a windpipe. Why so is a question for another inquiry.

Man's power of smell is in general inferior to that of many species of animals, and his apprehension of the objects of smell is inseparably bound up with and so confused by pleasure and pain. The sense of taste is analogous to the sense of smell, the only difference being that the sense of taste, by reason of being a modification of touch, is the more discriminating. Touch is the only sense in which man far excels all other animals, and it is by touch that he is the most intelligent of all animals. Flavours and smells can be divided into sweet and bitter, and they may also be pungent, astringent, acid, or succulent. In some things, flavour and smell have the same quality, in others they diverge. Bloodless animals do not breathe, and yet can still be said to have a sense of smell.

That which can be tasted can also be touched, and so cannot be perceived through an interposed foreign body. The thing that is tasted is suspended in liquid, and the resulting solution is itself tangible. Just as sight apprehends both the visible and the invisible (namely, darkness) and hearing apprehends both sound and silence, so taste apprehends both that which has taste and that which does not. That which is drinkable has taste, whereas that which is undrinkable tends to destroy taste. That which is drinkable is the common object of both touch and taste. Since that which can be tasted is liquid, the organ of taste must be non-liquid but capable of liquefaction without loss of its distinctive nature, for which reason the tongue cannot taste when it is either too dry or too moist. The species of flavour are the sweet and the succulent and the bitter and the saline, and also the pungent, the harsh, the astringent, and the acid. The organ of taste must be potentially of these kinds, and that which it tastes must have the power of making it that which it itself already is.

Is touch a single sense or a group of senses? Is flesh the organ or the medium of touch? The field of each sense is established by a single pair of contraries, light and dark for sight, acute and grave for hearing, bitter and sweet for taste, but in the field of the tangible there are several such pairs, hot and cold, dry and moist, hard and soft, and so on. In the case of the other senses, there are more than one pair of contraries, for instance, in sound not only acute and grave but also loud and soft, but in in the case of touch it is impossible to identify that which underlies the contrasted qualities and which corresponds to sound in the case of hearing. The flesh plays in the case of touch the same role as air in the case of the other senses. Whereas in the case of hearing or sight, we perceive because the medium produces a certain effect upon us, in the case of touch, we are affected not by but along with the medium. Flesh and the tongue are related to the real organs of touch and taste as air and water are to those of sight, hearing, and smell. Thus, flesh is the medium of touch, and the organ is seated inside. Just as sight has for its object that which is visible and that which is invisible so touch has for its object that which is tangible and that which is intangible.

This completes our account of the several senses. By a 'sense' is meant that which has the power of receiving into itself the sensible forms of things without matter, just as a piece of wax takes on the impress of a signet-ring without the iron or gold. By an 'organ of sense' is meant that in which such a power is seated. Despite having a portion of soul in them, plants cannot perceive, for they have no mean of contrary qualities and so no principle in them capable of taking on the forms of sensible objects without their matter.

Book 3

There is no sixth sense in addition to the five enumerated, not least because there is no special sense required for the perception of common sensibles such as movement, rest, figure, magnitude, number, unity. The senses perceive each other's special objects incidentally and all form a unity. For instance, the perception of the bitterness and the yellowness of bile cannot be the act of either of the senses, hence the illusion of sense, that is, the belief that if a thing is yellow it is bile. Man has more than a single sense because if not, there may be a failure to apprehend the common sensibles which go along with the special sensibles.

Does the awareness of seeing come through the sense of sight or through some other sense? The sense must be percipient of itself, or else there is an infinite regress. If to perceive by sight is just to see, and if what is seen is colour, then to see that which sees, that which sees must be coloured. There is indeed a sense in which the sense organ is coloured, for it is capable of receiving the sensible object without its matter, which is why even when sensible objects are gone the sensings and imaginings continue in the sense organ. The actualities of the sensible object and of the sensitive faculty are one actuality in spite of their different modes of being, but their potentialities are different, and one of them may exist without the other. Sense implies a concord or ratio, which is why, in the case of sight, excess of bright or dark destroys the sight. In the case of hearing, excess of sharp or flat destroys the hearing, and so on for the other senses. This is also why objects of sense are pleasant if they are brought into their proper ratio. It is clearly possible to discriminate, say, white from sweet, and also each sensible quality from every other, and the power that discriminates between them and the time of its exercise must be one and undivided.

There are two distinctive peculiarities by reference to which the soul is characterised, (1) local movement and (2) thinking, discriminating, and perceiving. Both speculative and practical thinking is akin to a form of perceiving, and, indeed, the ancients held that like is perceived by like. Yet, they ought also to have accounted for error, for the soul spends more time in the state of error than in that of truth. Perceiving and practical thinking cannot be the same thing, for the former is found in all animals and the latter in a few only. Moreover, perceiving and speculative thinking cannot be the same thing, for perception of the special objects is found in all animals and is always free from error (or admits the least possible amount of falsehood), while it is possible to think falsely. Thinking is part imagination and part judgement; imagination is different from judgement, for imagination lies within our power whereas judgement cannot escape the alternative of falsehood or truth. Imagination is neither sense nor opinion nor a combination or blend of the two. Imagination is a movement and impossible without sensation, and must therefore be a movement resulting from an actual exercise of a power of sense. Imaginations remain in the organs of sense and resemble sensations, such that animals in their actions are largely guided by them, some (the brutes) because of the non-existence of mind, others (human beings) because of the temporary eclipse in them of mind by feeling or disease or sleep.

What differentiates the part of the soul which knows and thinks (whether in definition only or spatially as well), and how does thinking take place? If thinking is like perceiving, it must be a process in which the soul is acted upon by that which is capable of being thought. This implies that mind must be potentially identical in character with its object without being the object. Other than having this capacity, mind can have no nature of its own, and is not actually any real thing unless it is thinking. Hence, it cannot be regarded as blended with the body, for then it would have some quality or even have an organ like the sensitive faculty: as it is, it has none. Whereas strong stimulation of a sense organ leads to its paralysis, thought about an object that is highly intelligible renders the mind more able to think about objects that are less intelligible, the reason being that, unlike sensation, mind is not dependent but separable from the body. Once the mind has become each set of its possible objects, its condition is still one of potentiality, but in a different sense from before. Flesh, for instance, is apprehended by means of the sensitive faculty, but the essential character of flesh is apprehended by something different either wholly separate from the sensitive faculty or related to it as a bent line to the same line when it has been straightened out.

In every class of things, there is matter which is potentially all the particulars included in the class, and a cause which is productive in the sense that it makes them all, the latter standing to the former as an art to its material. So it must be also with the soul. Mind as it has been described has the virtue of becoming all things, and there is another that has the virtue of making all things, a sort of positive state like light, which makes potential colours into actual colours. Mind as passive is destructible, but mind as active, when it is set free from its present conditions, is immortal and eternal.

The thinking of the simple objects of thought occurs in cases in which falsehood is impossible; if falsehood is also possible, then there is a combination of the objects of thought. Indeed, falsehood always involves a synthesis, and the assertion that that which is white is not white includes 'not white' in a synthesis. The word 'simple' has two senses, (a) 'not capable of being divided' or (b) 'not actually divided', and there is nothing to prevent mind from knowing that which is undivided, for instance, a length, and that in an undivided time. In this case, that which the mind thinks and the time in which it thinks it are divisible only incidentally and not as such. Points and similar instances of things that divide, themselves being indivisible, are realised in consciousness in the same manner as privations. A similar account holds for all other cases, for instance, evil or black, which are cognized, in a sense, by means of their contraries. Thus, that which cognizes must have an element of potentiality in its being, and one of the contraries must be in it. Anything that has no contrary knows itself and is actually and possesses independent existence.

Actual knowledge is identical with its object. Potential knowledge is prior in time to actual knowledge in the individual, but not in the universe, for all things that come into being arise from that which actually is. In the case of sense, the sensitive faculty is potentially that which the object makes it to be actually, and is neither affected nor altered. Therefore, this must be a different kind from movement. To perceive then is like bare asserting or knowing, but when the object is pleasant or painful, the soul makes a quasi-affirmation or negation, and pursues or avoids the object. To the thinking soul, images serve just as contents of perception, which is why the soul never thinks without an image. The thinking of an abstract object is just as the thinking of an actuality without the flesh in which it is embodied. In every case the mind which is actively thinking is the object which it thinks.

The soul is in a way all existing things, for all existing things are either sensible or thinkable, and sensation is in a way that which is sensible and knowledge is in a way that which is knowable. Within the soul, the faculties of sensation and knowledge are potentially these objects, the one that which is sensible, and the other that which is knowable. As they cannot be the things themselves, they must be their forms. The objects of thought are in the sensible forms, for images are like sensuous contents except in that they contain no matter. Imagination is different from assertion and denial, for true and false implies a synthesis of concepts; although neither primary concepts nor other concepts are images, they necessarily involve them.

The soul of animals possesses two faculties, that of discrimination by thought and sense and that of originating local movement. Is the part of the soul that originates movement a single part of the soul (either spatially or in definition) or is it the soul as a whole? The parts of the soul that have so far been mentioned are the nutritive, which belongs both to plants and animals, the sensitive, the imaginative, and the appetitive. The movement of growth and decay, being found in all living things, must be attributed to the faculty of nutrition and reproduction. Forward movement on the other hand cannot be attributed to this faculty, for this kind of movement is always for an end and is accompanied either by imagination or by appetite, and plants are not capable of originating forward movement. Similarly, it cannot be the sensitive faculty either, for there are many animals that have the sensitive faculty and that are yet incapable of originating forward movement. Nor can it be the imaginative or the appetitive faculty, for mind as speculative never thinks what is practicable and does not itself enjoin in pursuit or avoidance, and appetite can be successfully resisted by mind.

Practical mind and appetite appear to be the source of movement, and are capable of originating local movement. Appetite is relative to an end; the object of appetite is the stimulant of practical mind, and that which is last in the process of thinking is the beginning of action. That which moves is therefore a single faculty and the faculty of appetite, for mind is never found producing movement without appetite, but appetite can produce movement contrary to calculation. Mind is always right, but appetite and imagination may be wrong. Thus, the object of appetite may be either the real or the apparent good. That which is the instrument of the production of movement is to be found where a beginning and an end coincide as, for instance, in a ball and socket joint, with the convex side remaining at rest and the concave side being moved: they are separate in definition but not separable spatially. Just as in the case of the wheel, there must be a point which remains at rest, and from that point the movement must originate. To sum up, inasmuch as an animal is capable of appetite it is capable of self-movement. An animal is not capable of appetite without also being capable of imagination; although only some animals partake in calculative or deliberative imagination, all animals partake in sensitive imagination.

Can animals that have only touch have imagination or desire? Clearly, they have feelings of pleasure and pain, and so they must have desire. As their movements are indefinite, they have imagination and desire, but indefinitely. Sensitive imagination is found in all animals, deliberative imagination only in those that are calculative, and calculation involves making a unity out of several images. Though imagination does not involve opinion, opinion involves imagination. Sometimes appetite overcomes wish, at other times wish overcomes appetite, or appetite overcomes appetite. Thus, three modes of movement are possible. One premise or judgement is universal and the other deals with the particular, and it is the latter that really originates movement, not the universal, or rather, it is both, but the universal remains in a state more like rest, while the other partakes in movement. Thus, the faculty of knowing is never moved but remains at rest.

The nutritive soul must be possessed by everything that is alive, but not sensation. Indeed, touch cannot belong to those with uncompounded bodies or those which are incapable of taking in the forms without their matter. But animals must be endowed with sensation, for every body capable of forward movement would, if not endowed with sensation, perish and fail to reach its end. All things that exist by Nature are means to an end, and Nature does nothing in vain. If a body has sensation, it must be compound, for if it were simple it could not have touch, and without touch it could not avoid some things and take others, and so could not survive. That is also why taste, which is relative to nutriment, is also a sort of touch. Both these senses, then, are indispensible to the animal.

It is clear that the body of an animal cannot be simple, that is, consist of one element such as fire or earth. Touch is a mean between all tangible qualities, and its organ must be capable of receiving all the specific qualities which characterise earth, but also the hot and the cold and so on. That is why bones and hair, and indeed plants, which consist only of earth, are devoid of sensation. Excess in intensity of qualities such as colour, sound, or smell destroys the organ of sense, but excess in tangible qualities destroys not only the organ of sense but also the animal itself. Whereas sight, hearing, and smell are necessary to an animal's wellbeing, touch is necessary to its being.

CHAPTER 11

Sense and Sensibilia

Book 1

Having considered the soul and its several faculties, it seems appropriate to make a survey of all living things so as to ascertain the functions that are common to all or peculiar to some. These functions are attributes of soul and body in conjunction, for instance, sensation, memory, passion, appetite and desire in general, and pleasure and pain. These may be said to belong to all animals. In addition, there are other attributes, the most important of which may be summed up in four pairs, waking and sleeping, youth and old age, inhalation and exhalation, life and death. It also behoves the physical philosopher to understand health and disease insofar as these pertain only to living things. All of these attributes either imply sensation as a concomitant or have it as their medium, and it is clear – both by reasoning and by observation – that sensation is generated in the soul through the medium of the body. Whereas touch and taste are found in all animals, the senses that operate through external media are found in all locomotive animals. In such animals, these senses serve for preservation, but in animals that have intelligence they serve also for the attainment of a higher perfection. For developing intelligence, hearing takes precedence over seeing, even though rational discourse is only indirectly audible since it is composed of words, which are thought symbols. Nonetheless, it remains that those who from birth are blind are more intelligent than those who are deaf and dumb.

With regards to the nature of the sensory organs, inquirers usually take as their guide the fundamental elements of bodies, but find it difficult to coordinate four elements with five senses. They hold that the organ of sight consists of fire, since upon being pressed or moved fire appears to flash from it. But how does the eye see itself, and why does it not also see itself when it is at rest? The phenomenon of the flash occurs only when the eye is moved and when it is dark because only with rapid movement can the same object appear to be two, and only in the dark can that which is smooth naturally shine. If the eye really were fire, as Empedocles and Plato purport, why then can it not see also in the dark? It is absurd to argue, as Plato does, that the visual ray is 'quenched' by darkness. Democritus is right in holding that the eye consists of water, but not in holding that seeing is mere mirroring. The eye sees not because it mirrors but because it is translucent. In sanguineous animals, the white of the eye is fat and oily so as to proof the eye against freezing. This explains why, of all parts of the body, the eye is the least sensitive to cold. The eyes of bloodless animals are covered with a hard scale which gives them similar protection. It is senseless to argue that the eye sees in virtue of a visual ray that must extend all the way to the stars, or else go out to a certain point and 'coalesce' with rays emanating from the object. If one should explain the nature of the sensory organs by correlating each of them with one of the four elements, then the part immediately concerned with vision consists of water, the part immediately concerned with hearing consists of air, and the sense of smell consists of fire (for odour is a smoke-like evaporation that arises from fire). The visual and olfactory organs have their seat in the environment of the brain because the brain is the moistest and coldest part of the body, and cold matter is potentially hot. Indeed, these organs must be potentially that which their senses, as realised, are actually. The organ of touch consists of earth, and the sense of taste is a particular form of touch. Both touch and taste are closely related to the heart, which is the hottest part of the body, and the counterpoise of the brain.

In *On the Soul*, I treated of the various senses, but here I set out to determine that which each sensible object must be in itself in order to be perceived in actual consciousness. Light is the colour of the translucent, for whenever a fiery element is in a translucent medium there is light. Just as the bodies which contain 'the translucent' must have some extreme bounding surface, so too must the translucent within these bodies. Colour corresponds to this bounding surface, and is either at the external limit, or is itself the limit, in bodies. Light on the other hand is a nature that inheres in the translucent when it is without determinate boundary. However, the limit of a body is not a real thing, but the same natural substance which is also in the interior of the body. It is in fact the translucent, according to the degree to which it subsists in bodies, that causes them to partake in colour. Hence colour may be defined as the limit of the translucent in a determinately bounded body. That which when present in air produces light may be present also in the translucent in a determinately bounded body. If it is present, the body is white, and, if not, it is black. The other colours could be the joint product of white and black either juxtaposed or superposed in a certain ratio. The hypothesis of juxtaposition requires invisible magnitude and imperceptible time, so that the succession in the arrival of the stimulatory movements may be unperceived, and that the compound colour seen may appear as one. On the other hand, the hypothesis of superposition has no such requirements. Alternatively, the other colours could be the joint product of white and black blended together by interpenetration of their matter. This, and not juxtaposition or superposition, explains the existence of colours, for bodies that are interpenetrated appear to be one and the same colour from all distances alike.

Having spoken of sound and voice in *On the Soul*, it remains to speak of odour and savour, both of which are almost the same physical affection. In man, savour is more pronounced than odour, which in turn is less developed than in other animals. In contrast, man's sense of touch excels that of all other animals in fineness, and taste is a modification of touch. Water, although tasteless, is the vehicle of taste, either because (1) it contains in itself the savours, or (2) the savours are generated from it, or (3) some other agent is the efficient cause of the savours. As (1) and (2) are clearly false, it remains to suppose that water is changed by passively receiving some affection from an external agent. As a person washing colours in water causes the water to acquire their quality, so nature by washing Dry and Earthy in the Moist, and by filtering the latter, that is, moving it on by the agency of heat through the dry and earthy, imparts to it a certain quality which is capable of transforming the sense of taste from potentiality to actuality. The activity of sense perception in general is analogous not to the process of acquiring knowledge, but to that of exercising knowledge that has already been acquired.

The savours belong not to every form of the Dry but to the Nutrient, for neither the Dry without the Moist, nor the Moist without the Dry, is nutrient. Only composite substance constitutes nutriment for animals. It is qua hot and cold that food causes growth and decay, but it is qua gustable that it supplies nutrition, for all organisms are nourished by the Sweet. It is by the agency of heat that nourishment is effected by the Sweet, the other savours being introduced for seasoning to counteract the tendency of the Sweet to be too nutrient and to float on the stomach. Just as the intermediate colours arise from the mixture of white and black, so the intermediate savours arise from the Sweet and the Bitter. The savours which give pleasure are those that are mixed in a definite ratio. The taste of Sweet alone is Rich, while the Saline is very similar to the Bitter. Between the extremes of Sweet and Bitter come the Harsh, the Pungent, the Astringent, and the Acid. There are seven species of colour and seven species of savour. Just as Black is a privation of White in the translucent, so Bitter or Saline is a privation of Sweet in the Nutrient Moist. This explains why ash is so bitter, for ash contains no sweet moisture. The senses are liable to err with respect to percepts that are common to all the senses such as magnitude and figure, but not with respect to their proper sensibles, for instance, sight is not deceived as to colour, or hearing as to sound. In light of all of the above, it is evident that Democritus and most of the natural philosophers who treat of sense perception are wrong to represent all objects of sense as objects of touch, and to treat common sensibles as proper sensibles and *vice versa*.

Book 2

Translucency is predicated of both air and water, but it is not qua translucent that either is a vehicle of odour, but qua possessed of power of washing or rinsing and so imbibing the Sapid Dryness. Smell can take place in water as well as in air, for fishes are seen to possess the faculty of smell, even though water contains no air and fishes do not respire. Hence, if air and water are both moist, it follows that odour is the natural substance, the Sapid Dry, diffused in the Moist. The elements are inodorous because they are without sapidity, whereas wood and bronze are odourous because they are sapid. The natural philosophers think of odour as aqueous or fumid exhalation, but aqueous exhalation is merely a form of moisture and fumid exhalation is (a) composed of Air and Earth and (b) cannot occur in water. Instead, odour should be thought of as the influence of Sapid Dryness on the Moist that is present in both air and water. To put it differently, odour is in both air and water that which savour is in water alone. This explains why coldness and freezing render the savours dull and abolish odours altogether, for cooling and freezing tend to annul the kinetic heat which helps to fabricate sapidity. There are two species of odours: those that run parallel to savours and that are agreeable incidentally (in so far as the associated nutrients are agreeable if the subject has an appetite for them), and those that are agreeable in their essential nature, for instance, the odours of flowers. Of this species of odour man alone is sensible because his brain is larger and moister and colder than that of any other animal, and so more apt to be stimulated by odorous heat. The sense of smell occupies a middle position between the tactile senses of touch and taste and those that perceive through a medium, that is, sight and hearing. Indeed, the sense of smell appertains both to the tangible on the one hand, and to the audible and translucent on the other. Odour qua odour contributes to general health, but it does not, as certain Pythagoreans believe, contribute to nutrition.

If every body is infinitely divisible, are a body's sensible qualities also infinitely divisible? If this were not so, a body might exist without having colour or weight or any such quality, and therefore without being perceptible. On this supposition, every perceptible object should be regarded as composed of imperceptible parts, but such objects surely do not consist of mathematical and therefore purely abstract and non-sensible quantities. Moreover, by what faculty shall such quantities be discerned? Every object of sense-perception involves contrary extremes, and the intermediate lying between extremes must be limited. That which is continuous is divisible into an infinite number of unequal parts, but into a finite number of equal parts, while that which is not continuous is divisible into species which are finite in number. It is owing to the difference between potential and actual that the ten-thousandth part in a grain of millet cannot be seen or that a quarter-tone cannot be heard, even though the whole grain can be seen and the whole strain can be heard. Extremely small constituents are unnoticed because they are potentially but not actually perceptible, unless they have been parted from the wholes. The foot-length exists potentially in the two-foot length, but actually only when it has been parted from the whole. But objective increments that are very small, if separated from the whole, might fail to actualise and instead be dissolved into their environments. Such very small objects should nonetheless be considered to be perceptible, for they are potentially so already and destined to be actually so upon being aggregated. Since they can be aggregated to become actually perceptible, not merely as a whole but also apart from it, it must be that their sensible qualities are limited in number. That which is moved in space is moved from one place to another, such that there must be a corresponding interval of time in which it is moved. It follows that the movements proceeding from the objects of sense perception must arrive first at a spatial middle point between the sense organ and its object, as is obviously the case with odour and with sound. Even if acts of sense perception do involve a process of becoming (in that they form co-instantaneous wholes), the object is not perceived by the organ in virtue of some merely abstract relationship between them. Even though odour and sound are not bodies, they are an affection or process of some kind. This explains why they can be simultaneously perceived by the many even if they are emanating from a single body. But though odour and sound may travel, with regard to light the case is different, for light has its *raison d'être* in the being (rather than the becoming) of something and is therefore not a movement.

It must be assumed that, of two simultaneous sensory stimuli, the stronger tends to extrude the weaker from consciousness. Also that it is easier to discern each object of sense in its simple form than as an ingredient in a mixture. If two stimuli are equal but heterogeneous, neither is perceived: either there is no sense perception at all, or there is a perception compounded of both and differing from either, as when ingredients are blended together. For concurrent sensory stimuli to produce a resultant object, they must have contrary extremes of the same kind. It is impossible to perceive two objects co-instantaneously unless they have been mixed, for their amalgamation involves their becoming one. If they have not been mixed, the actualised perceptions will be two, and their perception is successive rather than coinstantaneous. Indeed, it is not conceivable to perceive two distinct objects co-instantaneously with one and the same sense. And it is still less conceivable to perceive co-instantaneously objects in two different sensory provinces, as for instance white and sweet. For the soul predicates numerical unity in virtue of nothing other than co-instantaneous perception, while it predicates specific unity in virtue of the discriminating faculty of sense together with the mode in which it operates. It is impossible to discern co-instantaneously contraries (such as white and black), or homogeneous sensibles that though not contrary are of a different species (such as the colours), or the components in compounds that are ratios of contraries, unless they are perceived as one. If co-instantaneous perception of sensibles in the same province of sense (such as white and black) is impossible, than that of sensibles in different provinces of sense (such as white and sweet) is a fortiori all the more impossible. Some natural philosophers assert that combined sounds do not reach us simultaneously but only appear to do so, their real successiveness being unnoticed whenever the time lag involved is so small as to be imperceptible. This can scarcely be true, for it is possible to perceive every instant of time; if not, a person might at any instant be unaware of his own existence, as well as of his perceiving. If the soul perceives white with one part and sweet with another, either that which results from these is some one part or else there is no such one resultant. But there must be one resultant, insofar as the general faculty of sense perception is one. That faculty does not perceive any one object, for no one object arises by composition of heterogeneous sensibles such as white and sweet. It must therefore be concluded that there is some single faculty in the soul with which it perceives all its percepts, though it perceives each different genus of sensibles through a different organ. Just as the same numerically one thing is both white and sweet, so the faculty of perception in general is itself numerically one and the same, but different in its being, different, that is to say, in genus as regards some of its objects, and in species as regards others.

CHAPTER 12

On Memory

People with a retentive memory are not identical with those who excel at recollecting; as a rule, slow people have a good memory, whereas quick-witted and clever people are better at recollecting. It is not possible to remember either the present, which is the object of perception or knowledge, or the future, which is the object of opinion or expectation. The science of reading the future may be called divination. When one has perception or knowledge apart from the actualisations of the relevant faculty, he can be said to 'remember' the object of perception or knowledge, either because he learnt it or thought it out for himself, or because he had a sensible experience of it. Memory therefore is neither perception nor conception, but a state or affection of one of these, conditioned by lapse of time. Consequently, only those animals which perceive time remember, and the organ by which they perceive time is also that by which they remember. The subject of 'presentation', without which intellectual activity cannot take place, has already been discussed in *On the Soul*. When one exercises the intellect, one envisages the object as quantitative and determinate. The intellect cannot be exercised on any object absolutely apart from the continuous, or even applied to non-temporal things unless in connexion with time. Magnitude and motion must be cognised by the same faculty by which time is cognised, namely, memory, and the presentation involved is an affection of the *sensus communis*, that is, the primary faculty of perception. Accordingly, memory of both sensible and intellectual objects involves a presentation and belongs directly and essentially to the faculty of sense perception, and only incidentally to the faculty of intelligence. Hence, memory can attach not only to human beings, but also to certain other animals. Memory appertains to that part of the soul to which 'presentation' appertains, and all objects capable of being presented are immediately and properly objects of memory, while those which necessarily involve (but only involve) presentation are incidental objects of memory. The process of sensory stimulation involved in the act of perception stamps, as it were, a sort of impression of the percept, just as a seal stamps its impression in hot wax. In those who are very young or very old, or too quick or too slow, or strongly moved by passion, an impression is less readily formed because the condition of their receiving organs is not optimal. When one remembers, does one remember the impression of the percept or the objective thing from which it is derived? A picture painted on a panel is at once a picture and a likeness; that is, while one and the same, it is both of these and can be contemplated as either. The same can be said of the mnemonic presentation within us, which by itself is merely an object of contemplation but in relation to something else is also a presentation of that other thing. Thus, it is possible to mistake memories for phantasms and phantasms for memories. In summary, memory or remembering is a function of the primary faculty of sense perception, that is, of the faculty that perceives time; it can be defined as the state of a presentation, related as a likeness to that of which it is a presentation.

Recollection is not the 'recovery' or 'acquisition' of memory, since at the instant of learning or experiencing one does not thereby 'recover' or 'acquire' a memory. It is only once the aforesaid state or affection is implanted in the soul that memory can be said to exist. To remember, strictly speaking, is an activity that only becomes immanent after the original experience has undergone lapse of time. It is obviously possible, without any act of recollection, to remember as a continued consequence of the original experience; only the recovery of the original experience can be said to be 'recollection'. Although remembering does not necessarily imply recollecting, recollecting always implies remembering. In some cases, a person may twice learn or twice discover the same fact, but this does not constitute 'recollection'. Recollection, as it occurs in experience, is due to one movement that has by nature another that succeeds it in regular order. As a rule, it is when antecedent movements have first been excited that the particular movement implied in recollection follows. Thus, when a person wishes to recollect, he will try to obtain a beginning of movement the sequel of which is the movement that he desires to reawaken. This explains why things arranged in a fixed order, such as the successive demonstrations in geometry, are relatively easy to remember or recollect. If a person cannot move, solely by his own effort, to the next term after the starting point, then this is not recollecting but forgetting. In some cases, he may set up many movements until he finally excites one of a kind that will have for its sequel the fact that he wishes to recollect. It follows that remembering is the existence, potentially, in the mind of a movement capable of stimulating it to the desired movement. From the same starting point, the mind sometimes receives an impulse to move in the required direction and at other times in some other direction. A person may think that he remembers when he really does not, but he cannot remember and think that he does not, for remembering essentially implies consciousness of itself. Remembering requires that the movement corresponding to the object and that corresponding to its time concur. If, however, the movement corresponding to the objective fact takes place without that corresponding to the time, or if the latter takes place without the former, then this no longer constitutes remembering. In some cases, the movement corresponding to time may be indeterminate, and yet remembering can still be said to occur. Recollecting differs from remembering not only chronologically, but also in that it is a mode of inference that can only belong to those animals with the faculty of deliberation, namely, man alone. That recollecting is a searching for an 'image' in a corporeal substrate is proved by the fact that people who are unable to recollect may feel discomfort. Melancholics and all those with moisture around that part which is the centre of sense perception feel this kind of discomfort very strongly, for once the moisture has been set in motion it is not easily brought to rest until the sought-after idea has presented itself. For a similar reason, bursts of anger or fits of terror are not easily allayed, and compulsions are not easily resisted. The very young and the elderly have bad memories because of the large amount of movement going on within them. The very young also have disproportionately large upper parts, as do dwarves, which predisposes to the skewing and dispersion of mnemonic movements.

CHAPTER 13

On Sleep

Sleep is a privation of waking and, inasmuch as they are opposites, sleep and waking must appertain to the same part of an animal. Moreover, the criterion of sense perception by which a waking person is judged to be awake is identical to that by which a sleeping person is judged to be asleep. If waking consists of nothing other than the exercise of sense perception, then the organ by which animals sleep or wake is the same as that by which they perceive. Sense perception is a movement of the soul through the body; as such, it is neither an exclusive property of the soul nor an exclusive property of the body.

Living things such as plants that partake of growth but that do not have the faculty of sense perception do not sleep or wake. Of those living things that do wake or sleep, there is none that is either always asleep or always awake. Organs lose power when they are over-worked, and so it is also with the organ of sense perception. It is impossible for any animal to perpetually actualise its powers, for which reason every animal that wakes must also sleep. Conversely, the faculty of sense perception exists to be exercised, and every animal that sleeps must also wake. Almost all animals have been observed to partake in sleep, whether they are aquatic, aerial, or terrestrial. Not so testaceous animals,[1] although

1   Animals with a firm, calcareous shell such as oysters and clams.

our reasoning leads us to suppose that they must do. By definition, an animal is any creature with sense perception. Creatures with sense perception also have feelings of pain and pleasure and consequently appetites, but plants have none of these affections. Since the nutrient part is more active when the animal is asleep, it is likely that sense perception is not required for growth and nutrition.

Some animals are endowed with all the modes of sense perception whereas others with only some. No animal when asleep is able to exercise any of the modes of sense perception. Each sense has something peculiar such as seeing or hearing, and something common whereby the person perceives that he is seeing or hearing. This common and controlling sensory activity chiefly subsists in association with the sense of touch, for the sense of touch can exist apart from all the other senses, but none of the other senses can exist apart from the sense of touch. As all animals are endowed with the sense of touch, they are all capable of waking and sleeping.

There are several types of causes, namely, the final, efficient, material, and formal. The final cause of sleep is the conservation of animals, which cannot continually be moving. The exercise of sense perception or of thought is the highest end for any animal, and this implies that (1) the waking state is the highest end for any animal, (2) sleep belongs of necessity to every animal.

As has already been demonstrated in another work, controlling sense perception originates in the same part of the organism in which originates movement. This locus of origination is one of three determinate loci, namely, that which lies midway between the head and the abdomen. In sanguineous animals, this corresponds to the region of the heart.

In sanguineous animals food ultimately turns into blood. Blood is contained in the veins, which originate from the heart. Sleep arises from the evaporation attendant upon the process of nutrition. The matter evaporated is hot and rising. Once it has risen to the brain, which is the coolest part of the body, it condenses and falls back down again to the region of the heart, resulting in sleep and then in dreaming. Thus sleep-inducing substances produce a feeling of heaviness in the head, as do fatigue, illness, and extreme youth. Awakening occurs once digestion is complete and the finest and purest blood, which is found in the head, has been separated from the thickest and most turbid blood, which is found in the lower extremities. Sleep resembles epilepsy in that it involves a kind of seizure that paralyses the primary sense organ and prevents it from actualising its powers. However, sleep is only one form of impotence of the perceptive faculty, which may also be made impotent by unconsciousness, asphyxia, and swooning.

CHAPTER 14

On Dreams

Sense perception and intelligence are the only faculties by which knowledge is acquired. As no animal when asleep is able to exercise any of the modes of sense perception, it may be concluded that it is not by sense perception that dreams are perceived. But neither is it only by opinion or intelligence, for in dreams it is asserted not only that some approaching object is a man or a horse, which is an exercise of opinion, but also that the object is white or beautiful, which requires at least some element of sense perception. In dreams as in waking moments, it is common to reason about that which is perceived – that is, to think something else over and above the dream presentation – and this too is an exercise of opinion.

The faculty which produces illusory effects during waking moments is identical with that which produces them during sleep. The sun may appear to be only one foot wide, but this illusion does not occur without actually seeing or otherwise perceiving something real. Even to see wrongly or to hear wrongly can only happen upon seeing or hearing something real. It has been assumed that sleep implies an absence of sense perception; it may be true that the dreamer perceives nothing, yet it may be false that his faculty of sense perception is unaffected. Thus, the senses may provide impulses to the primary sense organ, though not in the same manner as during waking moments.

Let us then assume that sleeping and dreaming both appertain to the same faculty of sense perception. In *On the Soul*, it has been established that the faculty of presentation is identical with that of sense perception, even though the essential notion of a faculty of presentation is different from that of a faculty of sense perception. Since presentation is the movement set up by a sensory faculty upon discharging its function, and since a dream appears to be a presentation, it follows that dreaming is an activity of the faculty of sense perception, but that it belongs to this faculty as a presentative.

The affection due to objects that produce sense perception is present in the organ of sense perception not only when the perceptions are actualised, but even when they have departed. Just as with projectiles moving in space, the movement continues even though that which set up the movement is no longer in contact with that which is being moved. So it is that, if one turns the gaze from sunlight to darkness, one sees nothing owing to the light still subsiding in the eyes. Also, if one looks a long time at one colour, that to which one transfers the gaze appears to be of that same colour. There are many other such phenomena.

As demonstrated by the case of mirrors, the sensory organs are acutely sensitive to even a slight qualitative difference in their objects. The eye in seeing is affected by the object seen, but it also produces a certain effect upon it. For instance, if a woman chances during the menstrual period to look into a highly polished mirror, the surface of it will grow cloudy with a blood-coloured haze. This stain is very hard to remove from a new mirror, but easier to remove from an older mirror. Thus, it is clear that stimulatory motion is set up even by slight differences, and that sense perception is quick to respond to it; and further that the eye is not only affected by its object, but also produces a certain effect upon it.

Let us then assume that the impressions of an object of perception remain even after the object has departed, and, further, that they are themselves objects of perception. Let us also assume that sense perception can be deceptive in the presence of emotions such as fear, desire, and anger. This explains why people in the delirium of fever sometimes think that they see animals on their chamber walls. The cause of such illusions is that the faculty by which the controlling sense judges is not the same as that by which it perceives. False judgements arise because appearances result not only from the object stimulating a sense, but also from the sense alone being stimulated in the same manner as by the object. Thus, to a person in a sailing ship it may appear that the land is moving, when in reality it is the person's eye that is being moved by the ship.

During sleep, owing to the inaction of the particular senses, stimulatory movements from causes within the body present themselves with greater impressiveness.

Like the eddies which are being ever formed in rivers, so stimulatory movements are each a continuous process, often remaining as they first started, but often being broken into other forms by collisions with obstacles. This explains why dreams do not occur immediately after a meal or in infants; in each of these cases, the violence of internal movement is such as to obliterate any sensory impressions, or to distort them into unhealthy dreams. Once food has been digested, the blood becomes calm and pure once again. This enables stimulatory movements to be preserved in their integrity and a clear image to be presented.

Not every presentation that occurs during sleep is necessarily a dream, for it is possible for the sleeping person to dimly and, as it were, remotely perceive light and sound and other external stimuli. Indeed, it is quite possible that, of waking or sleeping, while the one is present the other is also present in a certain way. Such occurrences should not be called a dream, and neither should the true thoughts, as distinct from the mere presentations, that occur during sleep.

CHAPTER 15

On Divination in Sleep

The divination that takes place in sleep, and that is said to be based on dreams, cannot be dismissed lightly. At the same time, it cannot easily be accounted for. It is claimed that the sender of such dreams is God, but this is difficult to reconcile with the fact that those to whom he sends them are not the best and wisest, but merely the commonplace. At the same time, none of the other possible causes appear probable.

Divinatory dreams must be regarded either as tokens or as causes of the events that they contain, or else as coincidences, or as more than one (and possibly all) of these. Even scientific physicians say that one should pay attention to dreams, and it is reasonable even for speculative philosophers to share in this belief. The movements which occur in the body during waking moments are generally eclipsed by waking movements. However, this is not the case during sleep, when even trifling movements seem considerable. For instance, dreamers fancy that they are affected by thunder and lightning when there is but a faint ringing in their ears, or that they are walking through a fire when there is but a slight warming over certain parts of their body. As the beginnings of all events are small, the beginnings of diseases or other bodily affections are more evident in sleep than in waking moments.

Neither is it improbable that some dreams are the causes of the actions which they contain. It is clear enough that potential or actual waking actions often shape our dreams, in which they may even be played out or repeated. In such cases, the daytime movements have paved the way for the dream movements. Conversely, it must be that dream movements can pave the way for daytime movements, and thus that dreams can shape our waking actions.

That having been said, most so-called prophetic dreams are mere coincidences, particularly if they are extravagant or remote in place or if the dreamer does not have any initiative over the dream content. In waking moments, it is common for a person to mention a thing and then to find that it comes to pass. Why, then, should such an occurrence not also be common in sleep?

Dreams occur in inferior people and in certain of the lower animals, and are neither sent by God nor designed for the purpose of divination. However, they do have a divine aspect as Nature is divinely planned, though not itself divine. According to the gambler's maxim, 'If you make many throws your luck must change', and so it is that people who are garrulous and excitable and who have many dreams are likely to have their dreams fulfilled.

That many dreams have no fulfilment is only to be expected, since another more influential movement could mean that that which is about to happen is not in every case that which is now happening. These beginnings from which no consummation follows are nonetheless real beginnings; they constitute natural tokens of certain events, albeit events that did not come to pass.

Some divinatory dreams do not involve the beginnings of future events, but are extravagant in time, place, or content, or are not extravagant but the dreamer does not have any initiative over the dream content. They may be a simple matter of coincidence, or they may result from distant movements that are perceptible to the sleeping soul. Such movements are more perceptible at night because then the air is less disturbed, and because people are more sensitive to slight movements during sleep than during waking moments. Divinatory dreams occur in inferior and commonplace people because their minds are derelict or totally vacant and so more conductive of alien movements. Divinatory dreams are particularly common or vivid in people who are liable to derangement because their normal mental movements are beaten off by the alien movements. People often have vivid dreams about those whom they are close to: just as acquaintances recognise and perceive one another from a distance, so they do with regards to the movements respecting one another.

Skilful dream interpretation calls upon the faculty of observing resemblances. Dream presentations are analogous to the forms reflected in water; if the motion in the water is great, the reflection bears no resemblance to its original. In such instances, particular skill is required.

CHAPTER 16

On Length and Shortness of Life

Of the animals and plants, some are long-lived and others are short-lived. Duration of life varies from one species to another, and, within a species, from one group of individuals to another.

Fire and water are reciprocal causes of generation and decay, and everything else that arises from them and is composed of them share in the same nature. However, many other things have another mode of dissolution that is peculiar to themselves, for instance, ignorance, the dissolution of which is called recollection or learning, and knowledge, the dissolution of which is called forgetfulness or error. The dissolution of a physical object leads to the dissolution of its non-physical reality. Thus, the death of an animal leads to the dissolution of its knowledge and of its health. The one exception is the soul, which does not admit of this kind of dissolution, and which therefore stands in a different relation to the body.

Something is indestructible if it has no opposite, or if, like fire in the upper regions, it does not meet its opposite. However, it is impossible for anything that contains matter not to have an opposite. A thing in which heat is present must be hot, or else attributes such as heat would have an independent existence. Whenever the active and the passive exist together, the one acts and the other is acted upon, and the result is change. This is so if a waste product is an opposite, and waste must always be produced, for opposition is always the source of change, and refuse is that which remains of the previous opposite. Once an opposite has been completely expelled from a thing, the thing does not become imperishable, but is destroyed by the environment. All things at all times are in a state of change and decay, but this process can be accelerated or decelerated by factors in the environment.

Immunity from decay is not related to size: the horse has a shorter life than man, and most insects live but for a year. As a group, neither plants, nor sanguineous animals, nor bloodless animals, nor terrestrial organisms, nor marine organisms, are particularly graced with longevity. The organisms with the greatest longevity are found among plants, for example, the date palm. Also with great longevity are sanguineous animals that have feet, for example, man and the elephant. As a general rule, larger animals live longer than smaller ones.

A living animal is humid and warm, but old age is dry and cold, as is a corpse. As organisms age, they become dry. Thus, the humid element must not be small, nor must it be cool and liable to congelation or desiccation. The warm element exists in different forms, for example, in the fatty substance of some animals. An organism that is to be long-lived must be humid and warm, and it must not produce too many waste products, which cause death either by disease or naturally. This is why salacious animals and those abounding in seed age quickly. For instance, the mule lives longer than either the horse or ass from which it sprang, and females live longer than males if males are salacious. Females also live longer than males if males are subject to great toil, which has a drying effect. However, all things being equal, males live longer than females because the male is a warmer animal than the female. Animals of the same kind live longer in warm climates because their larger size is a source of greater humidity.

Bloodless animals are shorter lived than sanguineous ones because they lack fatness. Marine animals are shorter lived than terrestrial ones because watery moisture is colder and hence more easily congealed. Animals and plants that are not fed consume themselves and perish thereby.

The organisms with the greatest longevity are found among plants, which are less watery and hence less easily frozen, and which have a certain oiliness that retains humidity. Plants constantly regenerate, springing up shoots and then fresh roots. Insects also live on through such a process of division, but their separate parts cannot produce organs and therefore cannot live for a long time.

CHAPTER 17

On Youth, Old Age, Life and Death, and Respiration

We must now treat of youth and old age and life and death, and probably of respiration as well, since in some cases living and the reverse depend on this. While it is clear that the essential reality of the soul cannot be corporeal, yet it must exist in some bodily part. All perfectly formed animals can be divided into three parts, that by which food is taken, that by which excrement is discharged, and that which is intermediate, called the chest or something equivalent. It is evident both by observation and by inference that the source of the nutritive soul is in the midst of the three parts since many animals, though divided, retain life in that member to which the middle remains attached. Divisible animals are like a number of animals grown together, but animals of superior construction behave differently because their constitution is a unity of the highest possible kind. In plants genesis from seeds and from grafts and cuttings always starts from the middle. Likewise in animals the heart is the first organ developed, and the blood is the final nutriment from which the members are formed. Hence, in animals the source both of the sensitive and of the nutritive soul must be in the heart, for the functions relative to nutrition exercised by the other parts are ancillary to the activity of the heart. If life is located in this part, then sensation must be too, for it is qua animal that an animal is said to be a living thing, and an animal is an animal because it is sensing. Taste and touch can be clearly seen to extend to the heart, and the other senses must also lead to it. The other senses are situated in the head, which leads some to think that it is by the brain that animals perceive; however, it is the central situation which is the natural position of a dominating power. The source of an animal's warmth is in the heart, which explains why death occurs when the heart becomes cold, but not when any of the other members do so. Hence, life must be coincident with the maintenance of heat, and death with its destruction. The life fire may be extinguished by a deficiency of nutriment or by excessive accumulation from lack of respiration and of refrigeration. Clearly, therefore, if the bodily heat is to be conserved, there must be some cooling method, just like the coals in a brazier must be ventilated if they are to remain glowing. In plants the natural heat is kept alive by the surrounding air supply and by their nutriment, for food has a cooling effect, and abstinence from food produces heat and thirst. Animals pass their life in air or water, and these media furnish the source and means of their refrigeration. All animals with lungs breathe, even though those with bloodless and spongy lungs have less need for breathing and can consequently remain under water for a longer time. On the other hand, animals with lungs charged with blood have greater need for breathing on account of the amount of their heat. Democritus, Anaxagoras, and Diogenes either imply or maintain that animals without lungs also breathe. Diogenes, for instance, says that when fishes discharge water through the gills, they suck the air out of the water surrounding the mouth by means of the vacuum formed therein, but this and other such theories are hardly tenable. The faults with these thinkers are ignorance of the internal organs and a failure to recognise that there is a final cause for whatever Nature does. Had they asked why respiration exists in animals, and had they considered this with reference to the gills and lungs, they might well have come to the correct conclusions.

Life and the presence of soul involve a certain heat. Not even digestion occurs apart from soul and warmth, for it is to fire that in all cases elaboration is due. For this reason also, the primary nutritive soul must be located in that part of the body which is the immediate vehicle of this principle, namely, that which is intermediate between that where food is taken and that where excrement is discharged. In bloodless animals this organ has no name, but in sanguineous animals it is called the heart. The blood in the heart and in the vessels that originate from it constitutes the nutriment from which the organs are formed. The other psychical faculties cannot exist apart from the nutritive (the reason for this having been given in *On the Soul*), which itself depends on the natural fire. This natural fire can be destroyed either by extinction through violence or excess of cold, or by exhaustion through excess of heat. In small and bloodless animals, refrigeration by surrounding air or water is sufficient to prevent exhaustion from excess of heat. If these animals are short-lived, it is because they have less scope for deflection towards either extreme. Some insects, though bloodless, are longer-lived as they have a deep indentation beneath the waist at which their membrane is thinner and so better adapted to the cooling function; the sound made by humming insects such as bees and crickets results from friction against the membrane caused by the rising and falling of air within the middle section. Sanguineous animals with spongy lungs can live a long time without breathing as their lungs, containing little blood, can rise to produce sufficient refrigeration. Among aquatic animals, those that are bloodless remain alive longer in air than those (such as fishes) that are sanguineous, since they have less heat and the air suffices to refrigerate them for quite some time. Sanguineous animals with lungs produce refrigeration by breathing air in and out, whereas those with gills do so by taking in water. All footless animals have gills with the exception of the tadpole, which has both gills and feet. No animal has yet been observed to have both lungs and gills; one means of refrigeration is sufficient in every case, and, as I am fond of saying, nature does nothing in vain. Every animal requires nutriment and refrigeration and, except in animals without lungs or with gills, nature employs the mouth for both purposes. Cetaceans such as dolphins and whales seem like a case apart, as they possess a lung and yet admit sea water. However, the admission of sea water is not for the purpose of refrigeration but of feeding, and these animals sleep with their head out of the water. Indeed, dolphins have even been observed to snore. After admitting the water they expel it through a blow-hole as fishes do through the gills. The higher animals breathe because they have a higher soul and a greater proportion of heat. Those with most blood and most warmth are of greater size, and man is the most erect as the blood in his lungs is the purest and most plentiful. The natural character of the material of an animal's body is of the same nature as the region in which it exists: water is found in water, earth on land, and air and fire in air. Thus, whereas the state of an animal's body can be opposed in character to its environment, not so the material of which it is composed. The source of life is lost when the heat with which it is bound up is no longer tempered by cooling. In time, the lungs or gills get dried up and become hard and earthy and incapable of movement, and then the fire goes out from exhaustion. In old age little heat remains and even a small disturbance can lead to death, which explains why dying in old age is painless. Generation is the initial participation, mediated by warm substance, in the nutritive soul, and life is the maintenance of this participation. Youth is the period of the growth of the primary organ of refrigeration, old age of its decay, and the prime of life is the intervening time. There are three separate phenomena related to the heart, palpitation, pulsation, and respiration. Palpitation is the recoil of the heart against the compression due to cold, pulsation the volatilisation of the heated fluid. When the hot substance increases it causes the organ to rise, which causes the outer air to rush in as into a bellows. The air's chilling influence reduces the excess of the fire, resulting in the contraction and collapse of the organ and the expulsion of the warmed-up air.

CHAPTER 18

Metaphysics

...for as the eyes of bats are to the blaze of day, so is the reason in our soul to the things which are by nature most evident of all.

Alpha

All men by nature desire to know. Thus, the senses are loved not only for their usefulness but also for themselves. Sight is loved best of all, for, of all the senses, it is the one that brings the most knowledge. Animals are by nature sensing, and from sensation memory is produced in some of them; these animals are thereby more intelligent and apt at learning than those that cannot remember. Those that have both memory and the sense of hearing can be taught, but the others cannot. Animals other than man live by appearances and memories and have but little of connected experience, but man lives also by art and reasoning. From several memories of the same thing man produces a single experience, and it is through this single experience that science and art are born. With a view to action, experience (knowledge of individuals) is not inferior to art (knowledge of universals), and men of experience succeed better than those with theory but no experience, for actions are concerned not with the universal but with the individual. Yet people suppose artists to be wiser than men of experience because artists know the 'why' or the cause, and can therefore teach, whereas men of experience do not know the cause and so cannot teach. Again, none of the senses are regarded as Wisdom because, although they give the most authoritative knowledge of particulars, they do not reveal the cause of anything. At first all the arts were admired, but with time the recreational arts (those that pertain to Wisdom) came to be admired more than the practical arts.

What are the causes and principles of Wisdom? As far as possible, the wise man knows all things, even though he may not have detailed knowledge of them, and he can learn things that are difficult and farthest from mere sense perception. He is more exact, more capable of teaching, and more suited to ordering than to obeying. The most exact of the sciences are those which deal most with first principles, for the sciences which involve fewer principles are more exact than those which involve additional principles. First principles are most truly knowledge, and also most knowable; from these all other things come to be known, but not vice versa. The science which knows to what end each thing must be done is the most authoritative, and this end is the good of that thing, and, more broadly, the supreme good in nature. As the good is one of the causes, this science must be the same as that which investigates the first principles and causes. That it is not a science of production is obvious even from the first philosophers, whose wonder brought them to philosophise. A man who wonders and who is puzzled thinks of himself as ignorant, and philosophises to escape ignorance and accede to knowledge, not for the sake of something else but for its own sake. Such a free science only God can have (or God above all others), and God himself is thought to be among the causes of all things and to be a first principle.

Evidently, then, we have to acquire knowledge of the original causes, and causes are spoken of in four senses (see the *Physics*). In one sense, a cause is the substance or essence, in another the matter or substratum, in a third the source of the change, and in a fourth the purpose or the good that it serves. Of the first philosophers, most think that the principles of matter are the only principles of all things. They argue that that of which all things consist, that from which they come to be, and that into which they are resolved (the substance remaining, but changing its modification) is the element and the principle of things; thus, nothing is either generated or destroyed in the sense that the substratum (or substrata) remains. Yet they do not agree as to the number and nature of these principles. Thales says the principle is water (a view that may have been shared by those who first framed accounts of the gods), Anaximenes and Diogenes that it is air, Hippasus and Heraclitus that it is fire, Empedocles that it is all the four elements, and Anaxagoras that it is (or they are) infinite in number. However true it may be that all generation and destruction proceed from some one or several elements, why do they happen and what is their cause? The substratum does not make itself change, bronze does not manufacture a statue, but something else is the cause of the change, and to seek this is to seek the second cause, namely, that from which comes the beginning of movement. Some of the first philosophers who hold that the substratum is one, as if defeated by the search for the second cause, say that the one and nature as a whole is unchangeable not only in respect of generation and destruction, but also of all other change. Those who admit of more elements are better able to account for the second cause; however, it is unlikely that fire or earth or any one element, or indeed spontaneity and chance, can explain why things manifest goodness and beauty both in their being and in their coming to be. When Anaxagoras and Hermotimus of Clazomenae first suggested that reason is present not only in animals but throughout nature as the cause of order and movement, they must have seemed like sober men. Perhaps Hesiod is the first to look for such a thing, and Parmenides and some others also think of love or desire as the first principle. Certainly, Empedocles is the first to conceive not only of an aggregative first principle which he calls love or friendship, but also of a contrary segregative first principle which he calls strife. Empedocles is also the first to speak of four material elements, even though he treats them only as two, fire as one kind of thing, and earth, air, and water as another. Leucippus and Democritus say that the full and the empty are the elements, calling the one being and the other non-being and making them the material causes of things. Those who make the underlying substance one generate all other things by its modifications; similarly, they make differences in the elements (namely, differences in shape, order, and position) the causes of all other qualities. All these thinkers evidently grasp, if only imprecisely, two of the causes which I distinguish in the *Physics*, namely, the matter and the source of movement.

For the Pythagoreans, all things seem to be modelled on numbers, and so they suppose the elements of numbers to be the elements of all things. Evidently, they also consider that number is the principle as matter for things and as both their modifications and their permanent states. According to them, the elements of number are the even and the odd, from which the One, which is both even and odd, proceeds, and number from the One. Other Pythagoreans say that there are ten principles, which they arrange into two columns of cognates, limited and unlimited, odd and even, one and plurality, right and left, male and female, resting and moving, straight and curved, light and darkness, good and bad, square and oblong. Alcmaeon of Croton also advances that the contraries are the principles of things, but how these principles can be brought together under the causes that I have named neither Alcmaeon nor the Pythagoreans can explain, although they do seem to range the elements under the head of matter. There are also those who speak of the universe as if it were one entity, but since they also maintain that change is impossible, the discussion of them is irrelevant to our investigation into causes. In summary, then, of the earliest philosophers, there are on the one hand those who regard the first principle, whether single or plural, as corporeal, and on the other hand those who posit both this cause and also the source of movement, whether single or dual.

In most respects, Plato follows these thinkers. In his youth, Plato became familiar with Cratylus and with the teachings of Heraclitus that all sensible things are in a state of flux and therefore that there can be no knowledge about them. Whereas Socrates seeks out the universal in ethical matters, Plato holds that the problem applies not to sensible things, which are always changing, but to the Ideas or Forms in which sensible things participate. For the Pythagoreans, things exist by 'imitation' of numbers, whereas for Plato they exist by 'participation' in Forms, but what 'imitation' or 'participation' involve they do not say. Moreover, Plato maintains that, besides sensible things and Forms, there are the objects of mathematics, which occupy an intermediate position. Since the Forms are the causes of all other things, their elements are the elements of all things. As matter, the great and the small are principles; as essential reality, the One; for from the great and the small, by participation in the One, come the Numbers. Plato agrees with the Pythagoreans that the One is substance and not a predicate of something else, and that Numbers are the causes of the reality of other things. However, he constructs the infinite out of great and small instead of treating it as one, and conceives of the Numbers as existing apart from sensible things.

The essence, that is, the substantial reality, no one has expressed distinctly. It is hinted at chiefly by Plato, who does not suppose either that the Forms are the matter of sensible things and the One the matter of the Forms, or that they are the source of movement. Instead, he advances that the Forms are the essence of every other thing, and that the One is the essence of the Forms. When the early philosophers speak of a cause, for instance, reason or friendship, they do not speak as if anything that exists came into being for the sake of it, but as if movements started from it. Thus, they both say and do not say that reason or friendship is a cause, in the sense that it is only an incidental cause.

Those who say that the universe is one and posit one kind of thing as matter, and as corporeal matter, only posit the elements of bodies and not of incorporeal things, though there are also incorporeal things. In giving a physical account of all things, they neglect the cause of movement. Furthermore, they do not posit the substance, that is, the essence, as the cause of anything, and call one of the simple bodies (water, fire, air) the first principle without asking how the simple bodies are produced out of each other, and so without considering their priority and posteriority. Empedocles posits that all four bodies are the first principles, but he can be criticised on the same ground and also on grounds that are peculiar to his position. The Pythagoreans do not say how there can be movement if limited and unlimited and odd and even are the only things assumed. It appears that they have nothing to say about perceptible things, for if spatial magnitude does indeed consist of these elements, how, for instance, could some bodies be light and others heavy? Moreover, is the number that is each abstraction the same number that is exhibited in the material universe, or is it another than this? According to Plato, both bodies and their causes are numbers, but intelligible numbers are causes whereas other numbers are sensibles.

Unfortunately, to posit the Ideas as causes is, so to speak, to introduce an equal number of causes to the causes. Besides which, there is no convincing proof for the existence of the Forms: from some proofs no inference necessarily follows, and from others there arise Forms even of things which are not thought of as having Forms. Of the more accurate arguments, some lead to Ideas of relations and others introduce the 'third man'. There are also other objections to the Ideas. Above all, one might ask what on earth the Forms contribute to sensible things, whether eternal or perishable, if they cause neither movement nor change in them.

Alpha the Lesser

The investigation of the truth is easy and difficult, easy in that everyone finds something right to say about it, difficult in that no one can attain it adequately. Perhaps too the cause of the present difficulty is not in the facts but in us, for as the eyes of bats are to the blaze of day, so is the reason in our soul to the things which are by nature most evident of all. It is right that we should be grateful to earlier philosophers, and it is also right that philosophy should be called knowledge of the truth, for, just as action is the end of practical knowledge, so truth is the end of theoretical knowledge. The principles of eternal things are most true, for they are not merely sometimes true, nor is there any cause for their being, but they themselves are the cause of the being of other things, so that as each thing is in respect of being, so it is in respect of truth.

But evidently the causes of things are neither an infinite series not infinitely various in kind, such that there must be a first principle. For neither can one thing proceed from another *ad infinitum*, nor can the sources of movement form an endless series. Similarly, the final causes cannot go on *ad infinitum*, in other words, one thing cannot always be for the sake of another and the other for the sake of yet another, and so on. And the case of essence is similar; in the case of an intermediate, the prior must be the cause of the later terms. However, in an infinite series, all are in a sense intermediate, so that if there is no first, there is, strictly speaking, no cause at all. One thing comes from another in one of two ways: either as the man comes from the boy, by the boy's changing, or as air comes from water. Although the former is irreversible and the latter is reversible, in neither case can the number of terms be infinite. At the same time, it is impossible for the first cause, being eternal, to be destroyed as in, for instance, in the case of water becoming air. If there is no last term, there can be no final cause, and the existence of an infinite series implies the elimination of the Good. However, the reasonable man always acts for a purpose, and the purpose, that is, the end, is a limit.

If the kinds of causes are infinite in number, then knowledge is impossible, for we think that we know only when we have ascertained the causes.

People have different ways of learning, and this can determine the method of inquiry. The best method for inquiring into things without matter is that of mathematics, but this method is not suitable for the material and changeable realm of natural science.

Beta

In this book, Aristotle 'surveys the difficulties' by presenting a number of metaphysical puzzles, for those 'who inquire without first stating the difficulties are like those who do not know where they have to go'. For each puzzle, he provides a thesis and an antithesis which can both be construed as an extreme answer to the puzzle. (1) Does the investigation of the causes belong to one or to several sciences? (2) Should such a science survey only the first principles of substances, or also the principles on which all men base their proofs? (3) If the science in question deals with substance, is it the only one to do so, and, if not, are they all akin? (4) Are there only sensible substances, or are there also others such as Forms and intermediate mathematical objects? (5) Is our investigation concerned only with substances or also with their essential attributes? (6) Are the principles and elements of things the genera or rather the primary constituents of a thing? (7) If the genera, are they the genera that are predicated proximately of the individuals or the highest genera; for instance, is the first principle and the more independent of the individual instance 'man' or 'animal'? (8) Besides matter, is there anything that is a cause in itself, can this exist apart, is it one or several, and is there something apart from the concrete thing (i.e. the matter with something already predicated of it)? (9) Are the principles – both those in the definitions and those in the substratum – limited in number or in kind? (10) Are the principles of perishable and of imperishable things the same or different, and are they all imperishable? (11) Most difficult of all, are unity and being, as Plato and the Pythagoreans maintain, not attributes of something else but the substance of existing things, or is the substratum something else such as love or fire? (12) Are the principles universal or like individual things? (13) Do the principles exist potentially or actually, and are they potential or actual in any other sense than in reference to movement? (14) Are numbers, lines, figures, and points a kind of substance, and if so are they separate from sensible things or present in them? 'With regard to all these matters not only is it hard to get possession of the truth, but it is not easy even to think out the difficulties well.'

Gamma

There is a science that investigates being as being and that is not the same as any of the other sciences such as the mathematical sciences, which only investigate the attribute of a part of being. The first principles and highest causes must belong to some thing in virtue of its own nature, and the elements of existing things must be elements of being not by accident but just because it is being.

There are many senses in which a thing may be said to 'be', but all that 'is' is related to one definite kind of thing, just as everything which is healthy is related to health in some way or another. Some things are said to be because they are substances, others because they are affections of substance, others because they are a process towards substance, and so on. Just as there is one science that deals with all healthy things, so there is one science that deals with all being qua being. Now science deals chiefly with that which is primary and on which other things depend; if this is substance, then it is of substances that the philosopher must grasp the principles and causes. If being and unity are the same in the sense that they imply each other, then there must be exactly as many species of being as of unity, and the investigation of their essence must be the work of a science that is generically one. Being falls immediately into genera, and sciences too correspond to these genera, such that there is a first and a second science and other successive ones just as there are, say, within the sphere of mathematics. The study of the negation or privation of the above concepts belongs to the same respective sciences, as well as the study of the contraries, the other and the dissimilar, the unequal, and everything else which derives either from these or from plurality and unity. It is evident that it belongs to one science to be able to give an account of these concepts as well as of substance, and, further, that this science is that of the philosopher.

Does it belong to a single science to inquire both into axioms and into substance? Evidently, the inquiry into these also belongs to one science, for these truths hold good for everything that is qua being. It belongs to the philosopher, that is, to him who is studying the nature of all substance, to inquire also into the principles of syllogism, and he must be able to state the most certain principles of all things. The most certain principle of all is that the same attribute cannot at the same time belong and not belong to the same subject and in the same respect (the principle of contradiction). Indeed, it is impossible for anyone to believe the same thing to be and not to be, and it is impossible that contrary attributes should belong at the same time to the same subject. Every demonstration can be reduced to this as an ultimate belief, for it is the starting point for all the other axioms.

Some thinkers assert that it is possible for the same thing to be and not to be, even though this is clearly impossible. Some demand that this impossibility should be demonstrated, even though demonstration of absolutely everything opens up an infinite regress and is therefore impossible. But if there are things of which one should not demand demonstration, then none is more self-evident than this one. First then at least this is obviously true, that the word 'be' or 'not be' has a definite meaning, for not to have a meaning is to have no meaning, and one cannot reason with words that have no meaning. Let

197

us assume that the name has a meaning and one meaning, in which case it is impossible that 'being a man' should mean precisely 'not being a man' if 'man' not only signifies something about one subject but also has one significance; and, except by virtue of an ambiguity, it is impossible both to be and not to be the same thing. Those who deny this do away with substance and essence since they must say that there is no such thing as 'being essentially a man', an expression which denotes the substance and thus the essence of a thing. However, the essence of a thing cannot be something else. Thus, they must say that there cannot be such a definition of anything, but that all attributes are accidental, in which case there can be nothing primary out of which anything is made. If the accidental always implies predication about a subject, then the predication must go on ad infinitum, which is impossible. Again, if all contradictory statements are true of the same subject at the same time, then all things must be one. Thinkers such as Protagoras who maintain that all things are one must also accept this premise, in which case they are speaking not of the determinate of being but of the indeterminate of non-being. There are also a number of other problems that arise from failing to recognise that contrary attributes cannot belong at the same time to the same subject. Above all, to do so and to be consistent is to say nothing at all, neither 'yes' nor 'no', but 'yes and no', and 'neither yes nor no'. Yet it seems that all men make unqualified judgements, if not about all things, at least about the better and the worse. If this is not knowledge but opinion, then they should be all the more anxious about the truth, just as a sick man should be all the more anxious about his health.

People think that contradictories or contraries are true at the same time because they see contraries coming into existence out of the same thing, and, indeed, Anaxagoras and Democritus both maintained that all is mixed in all. But 'that which is' has two meanings, so that in some sense a thing can come to be out of that which it is not, while in some sense it cannot. For the same thing can be potentially at the same time two contraries, but it cannot actually. Which sense impressions are true and which are false is not obvious, for many of the animals receive impressions contrary to ours, and impressions even vary from one person to another. This is why Democritus, at any rate, says that either there is no truth or to us at least it is not evident. And in general it is because these thinkers suppose knowledge to be sensation and this to be a physical alteration that they say that that which appears to our senses must be true. Empedocles, for instance, says that when men change their condition they change their knowledge. If even those who seek and love knowledge the most hold such opinions about the truth, it is no wonder that beginners in philosophy should lose heart. However, 'that which is' is not identical with the sensible world, which is largely indeterminate and constantly changing. If only the sensible existed, and if animate things and hence the faculty of sense did not exist, would there then be nothing? Admittedly, there would be neither sensible qualities nor sensations, but the substrata which cause sensations would still exist. Surely sensation is not the sensation of itself, and there must be something beyond and prior to the sensation.

One may well ask who is the healthy man, who is likely to judge rightly on each class of questions? This, however, is akin to asking whether we are now asleep or awake; one expects a reason for things of which none can be given, and the starting point of demonstration is not demonstration. If not all things are relative, but some are self-existent, then not everything that appears can be true; that which appears is apparent to someone, and he who says that all things that appear are true implies that all things that appear are relative. Thus, the most indisputable of all beliefs is that contradictories are not at the same time true of the same thing, and therefore that contraries cannot belong at the same time to the same thing (unless at least one contradictory belongs to it only in a particular relation, rather than without qualification).

There cannot be an intermediate between contradictories, such that of one subject a predicate must be either affirmed or denied (the law of the excluded middle). The intermediate between the contradictories is either like grey is between black and white, or like that which is neither man nor horse is between man and horse. In the latter case, it could not change into the extremes; however, an intermediate is always observed to change into the extremes, for there is no change except to opposites and to their intermediates. In the former case, there would have to be change to white which was not from not-white, which is impossible. In all classes in which the negation of an attribute involves the assertion of its contrary, there cannot be an intermediate; for instance, in the sphere of numbers there cannot be a number that is neither odd nor not-odd. While the doctrine of Heraclitus that all things are and are not seems to make everything true, that of Anaxagoras that there is an intermediate between the terms of a contradiction seems to make everything false, for a mixture is neither good nor not-good, and one could not say anything that is true.

Such doctrines destroy themselves, for he who says that everything is true makes the contrary statement true, and therefore his own not true, and he who says that everything is false makes his statement false. Against such doctrines, one must postulate not that something is or is not, but that something has a meaning and consequently that one can argue from a definition. Evidently, those who say that all things are at rest or that all things are in movement are not right, for if all things are at rest the same statements are always true or false, while if all things are in motion nothing is ever true and therefore everything is false. Again, it must be that which is that changes, for change is from something to something. At the same time, it is not the case that all things cannot be in perpetual motion or rest, for there is something that always moves the things that are in motion, and the first mover is itself unmoved.

Delta

In this book, Aristotle defines a number of key terms, often providing the several senses in which a particular term may be used. The terms defined include beginning, cause, element, nature, necessary, one, many, being, substance, same, other, different, like, opposite, contrary, prior, posterior, potency, capacity, quantum, plurality, magnitude, quality, relative, complete, limit, disposition, having, affection, privation, part, and whole.

Epsilon

I am seeking the principles and the causes of the things that are, qua being. All sciences that involve reasoning deal with principles and causes and inquire into some particular being or genus, but not qua being. They do not offer any discussion of the essence of the things of which they treat, but assume or hypothesise the essence and then demonstrate its attributes. Similarly, they omit the question of whether the genus with which they treat exists or not, and it belongs to the same kind of thinking to show what it is and that it is. Natural science is about one class of being, namely, that which has the principle of its movement within itself, and so is neither practical nor productive. If all thought is either practical or productive or theoretical, then physics must be a theoretical science. Of things defined, some are like 'snub' and others like 'concave', and these differ because 'snub' is bound up with matter (for what is snub is a concave nose) while concavity is independent of matter. As all natural things are analogous to the snub, it is clear that physics is mostly about substance as not separable from matter. Like physics, mathematics is a theoretical science, but some of its objects can be considered as immovable and separable from matter. If then there is something which is eternal, immovable, and separable from matter, the knowledge of it belongs neither to physics nor to mathematics, but to a first science that is prior to both. This first science may be called 'theology', since it is obvious that if the divine is in anything, then it is present in things of this sort. The first science does not deal with one genus, albeit the highest, but is universal because it is first.

The unqualified term 'being' has several meanings, one of which is accidental being and another true being; besides these there are also the figures of predication and that which 'is' potentially or actually. Regarding accidental being, there can be no scientific treatment of it; one who produces a house does not produce all the attributes that come into being along with the house, for these are innumerable. Plato was in a sense not wrong in saying that sophists deal with that which is not, since sophists deal above all with the accidental and the accidental is akin to non-being. The accidental is that which is neither always nor for the most part. For instance, cold weather in the dog-days is accidental, but not sultry heat. Or again, it is an accident that a man is pale but not that he is an animal, or that the builder produces health because apart from a builder he also happens to be a doctor. The cause of the accidental must be the matter which is capable of being otherwise than as it is usually. But while the usual exists, can anything be said to be always, that is, eternal? This is a question that I shall consider later, but as science is either of that which is always or of that which is for the most part, it is evident that there is no science of the accidental.

There must be principles and causes which can be generated and destroyed without ever being in course of being generated or destroyed, otherwise all things are of necessity, since that which is being generated or destroyed must have a cause which is not accidentally its cause. It is necessary that a man should die one day for in him some condition is already in existence, namely, the presence of contraries in the same body. However, whether he is to die by disease or violence is not yet determined and depends on the happening of something else, and that on the happening of something else, and so on. This process goes back to a certain starting point, which has nothing else as cause of its coming to be. The nature of the starting point of the fortuitous and the nature of its cause must be carefully considered.

Let us put accidental being to one side and move on to true being. That which is in the sense of being true, or is not in the sense of being false, depends on combination and separation (of subject and predicate), and truth and falsity together depend on the allocation of a pair of contradictory judgements. It is another question how it happens that man is able to think things together and apart, as a unity and without succession in the thoughts. However, it does imply that truth and falsity are not in things but in thought, and that the things that are in this sense have a different sort of 'being' from the things that are in the full sense. In summary, both that which is accidentally and that which is in the sense of being true can be dismissed as the causes and the principles of being qua being.

Zeta

That which is primarily is the 'what', which indicates the substance of a thing. When asked what a thing is, one does not say 'white' or 'hot' or 'three cubits long', but 'a man' or 'a god'. All other things are said to be because they are quantities or qualities or affections or some other determination of that which is in this primary sense. When using the word 'good' or 'sitting', some underlying substance is implied, and it is in virtue of this category that each of the other categories are. It follows that that which is primarily, not in a qualified sense but without qualification, is substance. There are several senses in which a thing is said to be first, but substance is first in every sense, (1) definition, (2) order of knowledge, (3) time. Of the other categories, none but substance can exist independently. The investigation of being is none other than that of substance, for it is substance that some assert to be one or more than one.

Substance is thought to belong above all to bodies, and all

natural bodies – animals, plants, the elements, and so on – and their parts are substances. Does anything else consist of substance? Some think the limits of body such as surface, line, and point are substances. Others think that there is nothing substantial besides sensible things, yet others (for instance Plato) that there are eternal substances which are greater in number and more real.

'Substance' is applied at least to four main objects, the essence, the universal, the genus, the substratum. The substratum is substance in the truest sense because it is that of which all else is predicated but is not itself predicable. Matter is said to be of the nature of substratum, as is shape, and also the compound of matter and shape, for instance, the bronze, the pattern of its form, and the statue. I have hereby outlined the nature of substance: substance is that which is not predicated of a stratum, but of which all else is predicated. This statement is rather obscure, and seems to imply that matter is substance. But this cannot be the case as both separability and 'thisness' are thought to belong chiefly to substance; form and the compound of form and matter should be thought of not as matter, but as substance. The substance compounded of both form and matter can be dismissed because it is posterior and its nature is obvious. And matter also is in a sense manifest. The inquiry into the third kind of substance requires an examination of sensibles, for one must start from that which is barely knowable but knowable to oneself, and try to know that which is knowable without qualification.

The essence of each thing is that which is said to be *propter se*, that is, specific to its very nature. Nor yet is the whole of this the essence of a thing; 'being a white surface' is not the essence of a surface, because 'surface' itself is added. Thus, the formula for the essence of a thing is that in which the term itself it not present but its meaning is expressed i.e. it is a definition. A definition does not consist in a word and a formula that are identical in meaning, but in a formula of something primary – primary things being those that do not imply the predication of one element in them of another element. The implication is that nothing that is not a species of a genus can have an essence. Essence and definition belong primarily and in the simple sense to substance, and only secondarily to the other categories – not essence in the simple sense, but the essence of a quality or quantity.

If a formula with an added determinant is not a definition, the terms that are not simple but coupled are not definable, as they cannot be explained without the addition of a determinant. A snub nose is a nose with a concavity, but snub and concave are not the same thing because it is impossible to speak of snubness apart from the thing of which it is an attribute *propter se*. Thus, either it is impossible to say 'snub nose' or the same thing must be repeated, 'concave-nose nose'. In either case, such a thing could not have an essence without opening up an infinite regress involving yet more noses. Clearly, then, only substance can be defined, and the other categories can only be expressed by the addition of a determinant, for instance, female cannot be defined apart from animal, or odd from number. Thus, there is at least one sense in which nothing has a definition and nothing has an essence except for substances. Definition is the formula of the essence, and essence belongs to substances.

Is each thing (substance) and its essence the same thing or different? With respect to accidental unities such as white man the two are thought to be different, for if not – if man and white man were the same thing – the essence of man and that of white man would be one and the same. What about with respect to self-subsistent things? If the essence of good is different from good itself, and the essence of animal from animal itself, then there are other substances and entities besides those asserted which are prior substances. If these prior substances were to be severed from their posterior substances, there would be no knowledge of them (knowledge being knowledge of essence), and the posterior substances would have no being. This indicates that each thing and its essence must be one and the same in no merely accidental way. In contrast, an accidental term such as 'the white' or 'the musical' has two meanings, referring both to that to which the accidental quality belongs and to the accidental quality itself; thus, there is a sense in which the accident and the essence are the same but also a sense in which they are different, for the essence of white is not the same as the man or the white man. Not only are a thing and its essence one, but their formula is one; unless this is so, an infinite regress cannot be avoided.

Of things that come to be, some come to be by nature, some by art, and some spontaneously. Everything that comes to be does so by the agency of something and from something and comes to be something which may be found in any category. Things that naturally come to be do so from matter, by something that exists naturally, and come to be a man or a plant or something of this kind, which are substances if anything is at all. That by which natural things are produced has the same formal nature which is specifically the same, for man begets man. Productions that are not natural are called 'makings', and all makings proceed either from art or from a faculty or from thought. Some of them happen spontaneously or by luck just as natural products sometimes do. From art proceed the things of which the form (the essence and primary substance) is in the soul of the artist. There is a sense in which even contraries have the same form, since the substance of a privation is simply the opposite substance. Thus, health is the substance of disease, disease being the absence of health, and health is the formula in the soul or the knowledge of it. Of the processes, that which goes from the starting point and the form is thinking and that which goes from the final step of the thinking is making. Obviously, some part of the result pre-exists of necessity, for the matter is a part and it is this that becomes something. At the same time, matter is also an element of the formula, for something like a brazen circle is described both by its matter and by its form. Though a thing comes both from its privation and from its substratum (that is, matter), it is said to come rather from its privation, and so the healthy man is said not to be an invalid but to be a man, and the man is said not to be health but to be healthy. However, if the privation is nameless, the thing is thought to come from its substratum; a statue is said to be not wood but wooden.

A brazen sphere is produced out of brass and out of the sphere; that which is spoken of individually as form or substance is not produced, but only the concrete thing, namely, the brazen sphere. In everything that is generated there is matter, and one part of the thing is matter and the other part is form. Is there then a sphere apart from the individual spheres? A form is a 'such' rather than a 'this', a definite thing; the whole, the 'this such', Callias or Socrates, is analogous to 'this brazen sphere', but man and animal to 'brazen sphere' in general. Thus, the cause which consists of the Forms is useless, at least with regard to comings-to-be and to substances, and the Forms need not, for this reason at least, be self-subsistent substances. In some cases it is even obvious that the begetter is of the same kind as the begotten, as in the natural products. The begetter is adequate to the making of the product and to the causing of the form in the matter. Callias and Socrates are different not in virtue of their form, which is indivisible, but in virtue of their matter, which is different.

Why are some things, such as health, produced both spontaneously and by art, while others, such as a house, are not? Some matter is such as to be set in motion by itself and some is not, and of the former kind some can move itself as required and some cannot. Thus, some things cannot exist apart from a maker or artist. Substance is the starting point of everything, and it is from 'what a thing is' that syllogisms can be formed. The form of substance does not come to be, and neither does the form of any of the primary classes such as quantity and quality and the other categories. However, in the case of substance, there pre-exists another substance that

207

produces it; in contrast, quantity and quality do not pre-exist other than potentially.

A definition is a formula and every formula has parts, each part of the formula corresponding to the part of the thing. Does the formula of the parts have to be present in the formula of the whole? The formula of the syllable includes that of the letters, but the formula of the circle does not include that of the segments. Further, if the parts are prior to the whole, then the finger is prior to the man, even though the finger can only be explained with reference to the man. If matter is one thing, form another, the compound of these a third, and the matter and the form and the compound are substance, then even the matter is in a sense called part of a thing, while in another sense it is not (but only the elements of which the formula of the form consists). Thus, flesh is a part of snubness but not of concavity. The formula of the circle does not include that of the segments, but the formula of the syllable includes that of the letters because the letters are parts of the formula of the form and not matter. Matter enters the concrete thing, but not also the form which is that to which the formula refers. 'A part' may be a part either of the form, or of the compound of form and matter, or of the matter itself, but only the parts of the form are parts of the formula, and the formula is of the universal, for 'being a circle' is the same as the circle and 'being a soul' is the same as the soul. Concrete things such as this circle (whether perceptible or intelligible) have no definition but are stated and recognised by means of the universal formula; in contrast, matter is unknowable in itself.

What sorts of parts belong to the form and what sorts of parts belong to the concrete thing? The form of man is always found in matter, namely, flesh and bones, even if these are not parts of the form and formula of man. Some say that the circle and triangle should not be defined by reference to lines and to the continuous because these are to the circle or triangle what flesh and bones are to man; instead, they reduce them to numbers, saying, for instance, that the formula of 'line' is that of 'two'. Some go further and make the number the Form of the line, or indeed the line itself. To reduce all things to Forms and to eliminate matter is useless labour, for at least some things are a particular form in a particular matter. An animal is perceptible, and cannot be defined without reference to movement and this without reference to the parts being in a certain state. If a hand is not alive it is not a part of man. Regarding the objects of mathematics, the formulae of the parts are not parts of the formulae of the wholes; this is not because the parts are perceptible things, but because they must have matter. Though the semicircles are not parts of the universal circle, they are parts of individual circles, and while one kind of matter is perceptible, there is another that is intelligible. It is clear also that the soul is the primary substance and that the body is matter, that man or animal is the compound of both taken universally, and that 'Socrates' can mean both the soul and the concrete thing.

The definition is a single formula of substance; as substance means a 'one' and a 'this', all the attributes of a definition must be one. With respect to the definitions that are reached by the method of divisions, it is the last differentia that are the form and substance of the thing and its definition. I am assuming that a differentia of a differentia is taken at each step, because if the divisions are made according to accidental qualities, for instance, if that which is endowed with feet is divided into white and black rather than into cloven-footed and not cloven-footed, then there will be as many differentiae as there are cuts.

It seems impossible that any universal term should be the name of a substance, for the substance of each thing is that which is peculiar to it, and substance means that which – unlike the universal – is not predicable of a subject. If not, many difficulties follow and especially the 'third man'. In complete reality, things that are two are never one, for which reason in complete reality a substance cannot consist of substances present in it. If no substance can consist of universals because a universal indicates a 'such' rather than a 'this', and if no substance can be composed of substances existing in complete reality, every substance must be incomposite and therefore without a formula. As it has already been stated that it is only or primarily substance that can be defined, this implies that there cannot be a definition of anything, or in a sense there can be, and in a sense there cannot.

The very facts make evident the problems that confront those who say that the Ideas are substances capable of separate existence, and at the same time make the Form consist of the genus and the differentiae.

Substance is of two kinds, the concrete thing (formula and matter) and the formula in its generality; substances in the former sense are capable of generation and destruction, but substances in the latter sense are not. However, without generation and destruction, formulae are and are not, for no one begets or makes them. For this reason, also, there is neither definition of nor demonstration about sensible individual substances; they have matter the nature of which is such as to be capable both of being and of not being, and this also explains why they are destructible. It is not demonstration and definition that deal with that which can be otherwise than as it is, but opinion. So when one of the definition-mongers defines any individual, he must recognise the limitations of doing so. Nor is it possible to define any Idea, for the Idea is an individual and can exist apart, but the formula must consist of words which are common to all the members of a class. For instance, in defining the sun the formula must be general, even though the sun is supposed to be an individual like Cleon or Socrates. If one of the supporters of the Ideas tried to produce a definition of an Idea, this truth would become apparent even to him.

Evidently, even of things that are thought to be substances, most are only potencies, both the parts of animals which do not exist separately and the elements which are not a unity but a mere heap. Since 'unity' is used like 'being', and the substance of that which is one is one, evidently neither unity nor being can be the substance of things. In general, nothing that is common is substance, for substance does not belong to anything but to itself and to that which has it, and no substance is composed of substances.

Since substance is a principle and a cause, let us pursue it from this starting point, for then perhaps we shall get a better understanding also of that substance which exists apart from sensible substances. 'Why a thing is itself' is a meaningless inquiry, since 'why' only has meaning if the existence of the thing is already evident. Thus, we are not inquiring why he who is a man is a man, but why something is predicable of something. Why are these bricks and stone a house? Plainly we are seeking the cause. While the efficient cause is sought in the case of genesis and destruction, the final cause is also sought in the case of being. Since the existence of the thing is a given, clearly the question is why the matter is some definite thing. – Why are these materials a house? – Because that which is the essence of a house is present. – And why is this thing a man? The reply consists of the cause, that is, the form, by reason of which the matter is some definite thing, and this is the substance of the thing. Evidently then, in the case of simple terms no inquiry or teaching is possible. That which is compounded, not like a heap but like a syllable, into a whole that is one is something other than its elements, and it is this that is the substance of each thing and the primary cause of its being.

Eta

Sensible substances all have matter. The substratum is substance, and this is in one sense the matter and in another the formula, and in a third the complex of these two which alone is generated and destroyed and capable without qualification of separate existence.

The substance which exists as potentiality, that is, as underlying matter, is generally recognised, but what is the substance which exists as actuality, that is, as sensible things?

There are many differences between things; it is necessary to grasp the kinds of differentiae because these are the principles of the being of things. None of these differentiae is substance, even when coupled with matter, yet they are that which is analogous to substance in each case. Just as in substances that which is predicated of the matter is the actuality itself, so in all other definitions it is that which most resembles full actuality. Obviously, then, the actuality or the formula is different if the matter is different. To define a house as stones, bricks, and timbers is to speak of the potential house, for these are the matter, but to define a house as 'a receptacle to shelter chattel and living beings' is to speak of actuality. Those who combine both of these speak of the third kind of substance which is composed of matter and form. From this it is obvious what sensible substance is and how it exists – one kind of it as matter and another as form or actuality, while the third kind is that which is composed of these two.

Sometimes it is unclear whether a name means the composite substance, or the actuality or form, whether, for instance, an animal is 'a soul in a body' or 'a soul'. As the essence attaches to the form and the actuality, this question is of no importance for the inquiry into sensible substance. The substance is the cause of a thing's being, but people tend to eliminate substance and state only the matter. Substance is either eternal or never destroyed; whether it can exist apart from the thing is not yet clear, except that this is obviously impossible in the case of things which cannot exist apart from individual instances, for instance, house or utensil. Indeed, it could be that none of the things which are not formed by nature are substances at all. One kind of substance, the composite kind, can be defined and formulated, but the primary parts of which this consists cannot be defined since to define is to predicate something of something, and one part of the definition must play the part of matter and the other that of form. If substances are in a sense numbers, they are so in this sense and not as numbers of units or points. They are numbers in the sense that (1) like numbers, they are divisible into indivisible parts, (2) their definition and essence changes if something is added or removed, (3) their definition is one although it is impossible to pinpoint what makes it so, (4) they do not admit of the more or less.

Even if all things come from the same or same kind of first cause, and even if they are all generated from matter, yet there is a matter proper to each, for phlegm the sweet or the fat, and for bile the bitter, or something else, though perhaps these come from the same original matter. It is also true that there may be several matters for the same thing, if one matter is matter for the other. When the matter is one, different things are produced owing to difference in the moving cause, but some things must have different matter, for instance, a saw cannot be made of wood. In speaking of causes, one should state all the possible causes, the material, the moving, the formal, and the final, though in the case of man the formal and the final causes may be one and the same. In particular, it is the proximate causes that should be stated, not, for the material cause, fire or earth, but the matter peculiar to the thing. In the case of natural but eternal substances another account must be given, for perhaps some have no matter or not matter of this sort. Matter neither belongs to those things that exist by nature but that are not substances, such as an eclipse. The formal principle is the defining formula, but this is obscure if it does not also include the cause; thus an eclipse is deprivation of light *by the earth's coming in between*.

Since some things, and in general forms, are and are not without coming or ceasing to be, not all contraries can come from one another, nor do all things have matter. How is the matter of each thing related to its contrary states? Is the same body potentially both healthy and diseased? Is water potentially both wine and vinegar? It is the matter of one in virtue of its positive state and its form, and of the other in virtue of the privation of its positive state and of its corruption.

All things that change into one another must go back to their matter, for instance, a corpse must first go back to its matter, and only then becomes an animal; vinegar goes back to water, and only then becomes wine.

What is the cause of the unity of a definition? What is it that makes man one rather than many, say, animal plus biped? If one element is matter and another is form, and one is potentially and the other actually, this question no longer poses any difficulty. For of things which have no matter, each is by its nature a kind of being and a kind of unity.

Owing to the difficulty about unity, some speak of 'participation', 'communion', or 'composition' because they are looking for a unifying formula and a difference between potency and actuality. But the proximate matter and the form are one and the same thing, the one potentially, and the other actually. As the potential and the actual are one, there is no other cause here other than that which causes the movement from potency to actuality. All things that are without matter are essentially unities and this without any qualification.

Theta

'Potency' has several senses, but potencies that are so called by an equivocation can be put to one side. Potencies that conform to the same type are originative sources of change, either in another thing or in the thing itself qua other. In a sense, the potencies of acting and of being acted on are one, but in another sense they are different, the one being in the thing acted upon and the other being in the agent. Insofar as a thing is an organic unity it is one thing rather than two different things, and so cannot be acted upon by itself.

Originative sources are present in soulless things and in things with a soul, and in soul, and in the rational part of the soul, so it is clear that some potencies are non-rational and others are rational. It follows that all arts, that is, all productive forms of knowledge, are potencies; they are originative sources of change in another thing or in the artist himself qua other. Non-rational potencies are capable of only one effect, whereas rational potencies are capable of contrary effects. For instance, the hot is capable only of heating, but the medical art can produce both disease and health. Indeed, a science is a rational formula which explains both a thing and its privation, even if there is a sense in which it applies rather to the positive state and to the negative state only accidentally.

Some say that a thing 'can' act only when it is acting, but this is ridiculous, for then a man is only a builder when he is building, something is only cold or hot or sweet or otherwise perceptible when someone is perceiving it, and something only has perception when it is perceiving. Again, if that which is deprived of potency is incapable, then that which is not happening is incapable of happening. 'Actuality' in the strict sense is thought be identical with movement, which is why movement is not assigned to non-existent things such as objects of thought and desire even though these may exist potentially.

Thus, it cannot be held that 'this is capable of being but will not be', even if it is not, for the false and the impossible should not be confounded. At the same time, it is clear that if, when A is real, B must be real, then, when A is possible, B also must be possible.

All potencies are either innate, like the senses, or come by practice, or come by learning. Whereas non-rational potencies are productive of only one effect, rational potencies produce contrary effects (although not at the same time, which is impossible). There must then be something else that decides, namely, the desire or will of the animal. It is important to note that an animal has the potency of acting not absolutely, but only on certain terms or conditions such as the exclusion of external hindrances.

What kind of thing is actuality? Actuality is the existence of a thing not in the way which is expressed by 'potentially'; it is as that which is building to that which is capable of building, or as that which is awake to that which is sleeping, and so on. All things are not said in the same sense to exist actually, but only by analogy, for some are as movement to potency, and the others as substance to some sort of matter. In contrast to many other things, the infinite and the void do not exist potentially in the sense that they will never actually have separate existence; they exist potentially only for knowledge. The process of dividing never comes to an end and so exists potentially, but not in the sense that the infinite exists separately. A movement that has a limit is relative to the end, whereas a movement that contains the end is a complete action. For instance, at the same time we are seeing and have seen, are thinking and have thought, are happy and have been happy, whereas it is not the case that at the same time we are learning and have learnt, are being cured and have been cured. Of these processes, one type consists of set movements and the other of actualities.

Earth is not potentially a man, but only when it has become seed, and perhaps not even then. If there is nothing in the matter that prevents it from becoming something, and if there is nothing that must be added or removed or changed, then the matter is potentially that something. If the source of becoming is internal rather than external, then the matter is potentially something if there is nothing external that prevents it from becoming that something.

It is clear that actuality is prior to potency, both in formula and in substantiality, and also, in one sense but not in another, in time. It is prior in formula because it is possible for it to be actualised, such that the formula and the knowledge of the actualisation must precede the knowledge of the potential. It is prior in time in the sense that the potential is produced for the sake of the actual, and the actually existing is produced from the potentially existing by an actually existing thing, for instance, man from man; in all cases, there is always a first mover which exists actually. And it is prior in substantiality because the things that are posterior in becoming are prior in form and in substantiality, and because everything that comes to be moves towards an end which is the actuality. Indeed, the word 'actuality' is derived from 'action', and points to the complete reality. Obviously, then, the substance or form is actuality, and one actuality always precedes another in time right back to the actuality of the eternal prime mover. Actuality is prior in a stricter sense also, since eternal things are prior in substance to perishable things, and no eternal things exist potentially. Thus, the sun and the stars and the whole heaven are ever active, and there is no fear that they may come to a standstill.

Whereas the capacity for contraries, for instance, health and disease, can be present at the same time, the contraries themselves cannot, which is why the actuality of health is better than the potency. In the case of bad things, the end or actuality is worse than the potency which is both contraries alike. This implies there is nothing bad in eternal things which by their nature are from the very beginning.

Iota

'One' has several meanings. The things that are not accidentally called one come under four heads, (1) the continuous, (2) the whole, and those things the definition of which is one and which are either (3) indivisible in number or (4) indivisible in kind. 'One', then, has all these meanings, the naturally continuous and the whole, and the individual and the universal. Above all 'one' means 'to be the first measure of a kind' and most strictly of quantity, for the one is the starting point of number qua number.

Is the one a substance, or does it have an underlying nature such as love or the indefinite? If no universal can be a substance, and if being itself cannot be a substance but only a predicate, clearly, unity cannot be a substance. In every class, the one is a definite thing, but in no case is its nature unity; just as in colours, the one is a colour, so too in substance the one is a substance. In a sense, unity means the same as being, since (1) it is not comprised within any category, and (2) to be one is just to be a particular thing, that is, to be one man is just to be a particular man.

That which is divisible is called a plurality and is opposed to the one. Indeed, the one derives its name and its explanation from its contrary, since plurality and the divisible is more perceptible than the indivisible and so prior in definition.

Things which differ may differ from one another more or less, and the greatest difference is called contrariety. For things that differ in species, the extremes from which generation takes place are the contraries, and the distance between these extremes is the greatest, and, as it is greatest, it is also complete. This being so, it is evident that one thing cannot have more than one contrary. The other commonly accepted definitions of contraries are also necessarily true. Every contrariety involves, as one of its terms, a privation, but not all cases are alike; in some cases, it is meant simply that the thing has suffered privation, in others that it has done so either in a certain part or at a certain time, which explains why in some cases there is a mean (there are men who are neither good nor bad) and in others there is not (a number is either odd or even).

Given that one thing has one contrary, how is the one opposed to the many and the equal to the great and the small? The word 'whether' is only used in an antithesis such as 'whether it is white or black' (not 'whether it is a man or white'), unless a prior assumption is made such as 'whether it was Cleon or Socrates that came'. The latter is not a necessary disjunction in any class of things, yet it assumes that opposites alone cannot be present together: if both Cleon and Socrates had come, then the question would have been absurd. Instead, the antithesis in question is that of the one or many, that is, whether both came or one of the two. If 'whether' is always concerned with opposites and it can be asked 'whether it is greater or less or equal', then what is the opposition of the equal to the other two? As it is contrary neither to one alone nor to both (but to the unequal) and intermediate between the two, it remains that it is opposed either as negation or as privation; and as it cannot be the negation or privation of only one of the two, it must be the privative negation of both. It is not, however, a necessary privation, for not everything which is not greater or lesser is equal, but only the things that can have these attributes. More generally, things that can be intermediate must belong to the same class and hence to the same substratum; that which is neither a shoe nor a hand need not be intermediate between a shoe and a hand.

Similar questions might be raised about the one and many. If they are absolutely opposed, then one is few (for the many are opposed to the few) and two is many, which is impossible. 'Many' is applied to the things that are divisible; in one sense it means a plurality that is excessive either absolutely or relatively and in another sense it means number, and it is in this second sense alone that it is opposed to the one. Each number is said to be many because it consists of ones and is measurable by one, and the one is opposed to the many as measure to things measurable.

Since contraries sometimes admit of an intermediate, intermediates must be composed or compounded of contraries, for (1) they must be in the same genus as the things between which they stand, and (2) they must stand between opposites of some kind.

That which is other in species is other than something in something, and this must belong to both, for instance, if it is an animal other in species, both are animals. It follows that the things which are other in species must be the same in genus, and that their difference, being other in the highest degree, must be a contrariety. To be 'other in species' is to have a contrariety, being in the same genus and indivisible.

Why then does male and female not differ in species? This is perhaps because the sex modification is less peculiar to the genus, with the contrariety being in the matter rather than in the definition. It follows that if a brazen triangle and a wooden circle differ in species, then this is not because of the matter, but because there is a contrariety in the definition. Male and female are indeed modifications peculiar to 'animal', but they are in the matter rather than in the essence.

Since contraries are other in form and the perishable and the imperishable are contraries, these must be different in kind. Some contraries such as pale and dark belong to certain things by accident, but others do not (in that they cannot not be present), and among these are 'perishable' and 'imperishable'. Thus, perishability and imperishability must either be the essence or in the essence of each perishable or imperishable thing. The characteristics in respect of which one thing is perishable and another imperishable are opposite, such that the things themselves must be different in kind. Evidently, then, there cannot be Forms, or else one man would be perishable and another imperishable. Yet the Forms are said to be of the same in form with the individuals, even though things which differ in kind are farther apart than those which differ in form.

Kappa

This book may not have been written by Aristotle. The material that it contains is repeated in other sections of the *Metaphysics* and *Physics*.

Lambda

If the universe is of the nature of a whole, then substance is its first part, and so the subject of our inquiry is substance. Substance is succeeded by quality and then by quantity, but these are not being in the full sense, merely qualities and movements of it. Indeed, none of the categories other than substance can exist apart. Today's thinkers tend to think of universals as substances, whereas the ancients thought of them as particular things such as fire and earth. There are three kinds of substance, one that is sensible (whether eternal or perishable), another that is immovable and that some identify with the Forms and the objects of mathematics, and a third that does not imply movement and that therefore belongs to a science other than physics.

Sensible substance is changeable, and change proceeds from contrary opposites or intermediates. This implies that there must be something underlying which changes into the contrary state. Something persists, but the contrary does not persist, such that there must be some third thing besides the contraries, namely, the matter. Change from one state into the contrary state occurs in each of the four respects of change, namely, the 'what' or 'thisness' (generation and destruction), the quality (alteration), the quantity (increase and diminution), and the place (motion). A thing can come to be incidentally out of that which is not, but all things come to be out of that which is potentially but not yet actually. All things that change have matter, even if this matter is not all the same. The causes and the principles, then, are three, the contraries of form and its privation, and matter.

Neither the matter nor the form comes to be, for everything that changes is something (the matter) and is changed by something (the immediate mover) and into something (the form). This process will go on to infinity unless there is a stop. Each substance comes into being out of something that shares its name, either by nature or by art or by luck or by spontaneity. Nature is a principle of movement in the thing itself, art in the something other, and the other causes are privations of these two. There are three kinds of substance, the matter, the nature, and the particular substance composed of these two. In some cases, the 'this' does not exist apart from the composite substance; if the 'this' exists apart from the concrete thing, it is only in the case of natural objects. Thus Plato was not far wrong in holding that there are as many Forms as there are kinds of natural object (if indeed there are Forms distinct from the things of this earth). The moving causes exist as things preceding the effects, but causes in the sense of definitions are simultaneous with their effects. Evidently, then, there is no necessity for the existence of Ideas.

The causes and principles of different things are different in one sense and in another sense they are the same for all. Are the principles and elements different or the same for substances and relative terms, and for each of the categories? If they are the same for all, then the same elements should yield both relative terms and substances, which is impossible. If all things can be said to have the same elements, then this is only analogically in the sense that one might say that there are three principles, the form, the privation, and the matter. But each of these is different for each class. Causes include not only the elements present in a thing, but also something external, namely, the moving cause. Analogically there are three elements but four causes and principles, even though the elements are different in different things, and the proximate moving cause is different for different things.

> *Health, disease, body; the moving cause is the medical art. Form, disorder of a particular kind, bricks; the moving cause is the building art. And since the moving cause in the case of natural things is-for man, for instance, man, and in the products of thought the form or its contrary, there will be in a sense three causes, while in a sense there are four. For the medical art is in some sense health, and the building art is the form of the house, and man begets man; further, besides these there is that which as first of all things moves all things.*[1]

Some things can exist apart and some cannot, and only the former are substances. Therefore all things have the same causes because, without substances, modifications and movements cannot exist. In another sense, analogically identical things are principles i.e. actuality and potentiality, but these are different for different things and apply in different ways to them. The proximate principles of all things

1   Translated by WD Ross.

are the 'this' which is proximate in actuality and another which is proximate in potentiality. Thus, the originative principle of the individual is the individual, such that universal causes do not exist. Man is the originative principle of man universally, but there is no universal man. If the causes of substances are the causes of all things, and yet different things have different causes and elements, then the causes of things that are not in the same class are different except in an analogical sense; and those of things that are in the same species are different except in a universal sense. The causes of all things are the same only in the sense that (1) matter, form, privation, and the moving cause are common to all things, (2) the causes of substances are the causes of all things, (3) that which is first in respect of complete reality is the cause of all things.

Of the three kinds of substance, two of them are physical and one unmovable, and it is necessary for the latter to be eternal. If all substances were destructible, then all things would be destructible, and movement and time would never have come into being (for movement must always have existed). Movement is continuous in the sense in which time is, and time is either the same thing as movement or an attribute of movement. There is no continuous movement except circular movement in place. Potency would not be exercised and there would be no movement if that which is capable of moving things did not do so, for which reason there must be a principle whose very essence is actuality. To suppose that potentiality is prior to actuality is in one sense right and in another sense not, for generation and destruction would be impossible without something else that is always acting in different ways. This something else must act in one way in virtue of itself and in another in virtue of something else, either a third agent or the first. And it must be the first, or else it causes the motion both of the second agent and of the third. The first was the cause of eternal uniformity, and something else is the cause of variety, and both together are the cause of eternal variety.

There is, then, something which is always moved with an unceasing circular motion, and something which moves this first heaven without itself being moved, and which is eternal, substance, and actuality. The object of desire and the object of thought move without being moved, and their primary objects are the same. A final cause may exist among unchangeable entities, for the final cause is (1) some being for whose good an action is done, and (2) something at which the action aims. The final cause, then, produces motion as being loved, but all other things move by being moved. Something that moves itself while being unmoved and existing actually cannot change and is not therefore subject to spatial motion. In so far as the first mover exists by necessity, its mode of being is good, and in this sense it is a first principle. It is a life such as the best that man enjoys, for its actuality is also pleasure, and so waking, perception, and thinking are all most pleasant. Thought thinks on itself because it shares the nature of the object of thought, becoming an object of thought upon coming into contact with and thinking its objects. That which is capable of receiving the object of thought, that is, the essence, is itself thought, but is active when it possesses this object. It is the possession rather than the receptivity that is the divine element of thought, and the act of contemplation is best and most pleasant. God is always in that good state in which man sometimes is, indeed in a better state, which compels our wonder.

> *And life also belongs to God; for the actuality of thought is life, and God is that actuality; and God's self-dependent actuality is life most good and eternal. We say therefore that God is a living being, eternal, most good, so that life and duration continuous and eternal belong to God; for this is God.*

Those who suppose that beauty and goodness are not present in the beginning but in the effects of the causes are mistaken, for the seed comes from other individuals that are prior and complete, such that the first thing is not the seed but the complete being. It is clear, then, that there is a substance that is all of eternal, unmovable, separate, without magnitude or parts, indivisible, impassive, and unalterable.

Evidently there is but one heaven; if not, the moving principles will be one in form but many in number, and things that are many in number have matter whereas the primary essence, being a complete reality, does not have matter. Besides the simple spatial movement of the universe which the first and unmovable substance produces, there are other spatial movements. The movement of the planets also are circular and eternal, and also must be caused by a substance that is both unmovable and eternal. The planets are moved by either 47 or 55 interconnected spheres which form a unified planetary system with the earth at their centre.

The divine thought thinks of that which is most divine and precious and of nothing else, for to think of something else would be change for the worse, and would constitute a movement. Since it is the most excellent of things, the divine thought must be of itself, and its thinking is a thinking on thinking. If the act of thinking and the object of thought are not the same thing, in the productive sciences the knowledge is the object of thought (the substance or essence of the object, matter omitted), and in the theoretical sciences it is the act of thinking (the definition). Since thought and the object of thought are not different in the case of things that do not have matter, the divine thought and its object are one and the same.

The nature of the universe contains the good probably both as something separate and as the order of its parts. All other things are confronted by the necessary consequence that there is something contrary to wisdom or the highest knowledge, but there is nothing contrary to that which is primary, for all contraries have matter, and things that have matter exist only potentially.

Mu & Nu

Books Mu and Nu concern the philosophy of mathematics, and in particular how it is that numbers exist.

It is said that the objects of mathematics are substances, and again that the Ideas are substances. Do the objects of mathematics exist, and if so, how? If they do exist, then they must exist either in sensible objects or separate from sensible objects. If neither, then they do not exist or they exist only in some special sense.

It is impossible for mathematical objects to exist in sensible things as it is impossible for two solids to be in the same place. Furthermore, if sensible things containing mathematical objects were to be divided, so too would the mathematical objects. And yet mathematical objects can neither exist separately, for then there would need to be planes and lines and points separate from those in the sensible solids and prior to them, for which there would need to be yet more planes and lines and points – which is absurd. And the same account applies also to numbers. If one thing is able to exist apart from sensible things, then all the objects of sense might also be able to exist apart from sensible things. In virtue of what will mathematical magnitudes hold together as one rather than divide into any number of quantities? The solid, having completeness, is a sort of substance, but lines and points cannot be substances, neither as form nor as matter, since nothing can be put together out of lines or points. The result of abstraction is not necessarily prior, and the result of adding determinants posterior, for it is by adding a determinant to pale that the pale man can be spoken of. Thus, it appears that the objects of mathematics either do not exist at all or exist but only in a special sense.

Propositions and demonstrations are about sensible magnitudes not qua sensible but qua possessed of certain definite qualities. Just as things which are inseparable exist, so the objects of mathematics exist. However, mathematics does not treat of them qua sensible, and so is not a science of sensibles – but neither is it a science of other things separable from sensibles. A science which abstracts from spatial magnitude is more precise than one which takes it into account; the most precise of sciences abstracts from movement or is concerned only with primary movement. The same account may be given of harmonics and optics; neither considers its objects qua sight or qua voice, but qua lines and numbers which are attributes proper to sight and voice. Each question is best investigated by separating that which is not separate, as the mathematician does. The good and the beautiful differ in that the former implies conduct as its subject while the latter is found also in motionless things. The chief forms of beauty are order and symmetry and definiteness, which mathematics demonstrates in a special degree. As these (order, symmetry, the beautiful) are causes of many things, mathematics also treats of this sort of cause qua cause.

The existence of Ideas was posited so that knowledge or thought might have objects that are not in a state of flux. However, of the ways in which it is proved that the Forms exist, none is convincing: from some no inference necessarily follows, and from some there arise Forms even of things that seem unlikely to have Forms. Of the most accurate arguments, some lead to Ideas of relations and others introduce the 'third man'. If the Forms can be shared in, then they must be of substances only, for they must be shared in not incidentally but as something not predicated of a subject. However, the same names indicate substance in this and in the ideal world, and if they both have the same form, then there will be something common. If the common definitions apply to the Forms and 'what really is' has to be added, then to which part or parts of the definition does it have to be added?

As the Forms cause neither movement nor change, they do not appear to contribute to sensible things. As they are not the substance of other things, they do not help towards their being or knowledge. Moreover, all other things cannot come from the Forms in the usual senses of 'from': whether Socrates exists or not, a man like Socrates might come to be. As there may be several patterns of the same thing, the same thing might correspond to several Forms, and these Forms in turn might correspond to further Forms, such that the same thing might be both pattern and copy. Things do not come into being unless there is something to originate movement, and many things, such as a house or ring, come into being despite not having been attributed Forms.

Some say that numbers are separable substances and first causes of things. All who say the 1 is an element and principle of things suppose numbers to consist of abstract units, except the Pythagoreans who suppose them to have magnitude. Such numbers may be described in one of several ways, some being more impossible than others.

Are the units associable or not? If all units are associable and without difference, then this is mathematical (rather than ideal) number – only one kind of number. The Ideas could not be the numbers, for what sort of number would man-himself or animal-itself or any other Form be? There is one Idea of each thing, but the similar and undifferentiated numbers are infinitely many. But if the Ideas are not numbers, then they cannot exist at all, for what principles would they come from? If the units are not associable, then they cannot be mathematical number but nor can they be ideal number, for 2 could not proceed immediately from 1 and the indefinite dyad, and be followed by the successive numbers.

By the Same Author

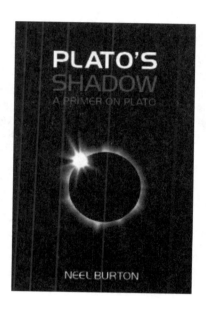

Plato's Shadow – A Primer on Plato

Plato thought that only philosophy could bring true understanding, since it alone examines the presuppositions and assumptions that other subjects merely take for granted. He conceived of philosophy as a single discipline defined by a distinctive intellectual method, and capable of carrying human thought far beyond the realms of common sense or everyday experience. The unrivalled scope and incisiveness of his writings as well as their enduring aesthetic and emotional appeal have captured the hearts and minds of generation after generation of readers. Unlike the thinkers who came before him, Plato never spoke with his own voice. Instead, he presented readers with a variety of perspectives to engage with, leaving them free to reach their own, sometimes radically different, conclusions. 'No one,' he said, 'ever teaches well who wants to teach, or governs well who wants to govern.'

This book provides the student and general reader with a comprehensive overview of Plato's thought. It includes an introduction to the life and times of Plato and – for the first time – a précis of each of his dialogues, among which the Apology, Laches, Gorgias, Symposium, Phaedrus, Phaedo, Meno, Timaeus, Theaetetus, Republic, and 17 others.

The Meaning of Madness

This book proposes to open up the debate on mental disorders, to get people interested and talking, and to get them thinking. For example, what is schizophrenia? Why is it so common? Why does it affect human beings and not animals? What might this tell us about our mind and body, language and creativity, music and religion? What are the boundaries between mental disorder and 'normality'? Is there a relationship between mental disorder and genius? These are some of the difficult but important questions that this book confronts, with the overarching aim of exploring what mental disorders can teach us about human nature and the human condition.

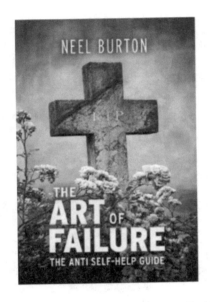

The Art of Failure, The Anti Self-Help Guide

We spend most of our time and energy chasing success, such that we have little left over for thinking and feeling, being and relating. As a result, we fail in the deepest possible way. We fail as human beings.

The Art of Failure explores what it means to be successful, and how, if at all, true success can be achieved.

Index